THE HANDS-ON GUIDE TO
SCHOOL
IMPROVEMENT

Transform Culture,
Empower Teachers, and
Raise Student Achievement

Evelyn M. Randle-Robbins, M.A.

Edited by Al Desetta

free spirit
PUBLISHING®

Library of Congress Cataloging-in-Publication Data
Names: Randle-Robbins, Evelyn M., author.
Title: The hands-on guide to school improvement : transform culture, empower teachers, and raise student achievement / by Evelyn M. Randle-Robbins, M.A. ; edited by Al Desetta.
Description: Golden Valley, MN : Free Spirit Publishing, 2016. | Includes index.
Identifiers: LCCN 2015040151 (print) | LCCN 2015051407 (ebook) | ISBN 9781631980251 (paperback) | ISBN 1631980254 (paperback) | ISBN 9781631980725 (Web pdf) | ISBN 9781631980732 (epub)
Subjects: LCSH: School improvement programs—United States. | School management and organization—United States. | Educational leadership—United States. | Communication in education—United States. | Teachers—In-service training—United States. | Effective teaching—United States. | School environment—United States. | BISAC: EDUCATION / Administration / General. | EDUCATION / Leadership.
Classification: LCC LB2822.82 .R385 2016 (print) | LCC LB2822.82 (ebook) | DDC 371.2/07—dc23
LC record available at http://lccn.loc.gov/2015040151

Edited by Al Desetta and Alison Behnke
Cover and interior design by Emily Dyer

10 9 8 7 6 5 4 3 2 1
Printed in the United States of America

Free Spirit Publishing Inc.
6325 Sandburg Road, Suite 100
Golden Valley, MN 55427-3674
(612) 338-2068
help4kids@freespirit.com
www.freespirit.com

Free Spirit offers competitive pricing.
Contact edsales@freespirit.com for pricing information on multiple quantity purchases.

I dedicate this book to Chris and Kennedi for sharing me and my time with students, teachers, and families; and to my mother for teaching me Proverbs 3:5–6.

Contents

List of Figures

List of Reproducible Forms

These forms can be downloaded and printed at
www.freespirit.com/HG2SI-forms. *Use password **4change**.*

Introduction

The Hands-On Guide to School Improvement is a practical, no-nonsense book that will help principals and administrators bring transformational change to their schools—whatever their needs, strengths, goals, or starting points are. The hard-earned advice in this book is based on my more than twenty years of experience as a teacher, assistant principal, and principal in Chicago Public Schools. In these pages you will find insights, recommendations, and practical applications that will dramatically improve school culture, transform teaching, and boost student achievement.

Many books have been written about school improvement and leadership. However, few are written by active school principals. This book is not based on research I've conducted about schools or on interviews with educators. Instead, it offers something more concrete and direct—a first-person account of my ongoing work as an instructional leader. I have been responsible for every detail of school leadership: from greeting students when they arrive in the morning, to creating a culture of respect and harmony, to monitoring teachers in the classroom, to improving schoolwide academic achievement. Everything I recommend in this book has been tried and tested in the day-to-day realities of challenging school environments. And while my experience comes from schools that were once struggling, the lessons in this book apply to any school, in any community.

Consider the following statistics: In 2013, only 41 percent of U.S. public school students in fourth grade and only 34 percent in eighth grade performed at or above proficiency in mathematics. In the same year, only 34 percent of U.S. public school students performed at or above proficiency in reading in both fourth and eighth grades, with the percentages in the states ranging from 17 percent to 48 percent. For twelfth graders, the news was even worse: only 26 percent of high school seniors in 2013 were at or above proficiency in math, and 38 percent were at or above proficiency in reading.[1]

---

[1] National Assessment of Educational Progress, "2013 Mathematics and Reading," *The Nation's Report Card,* 2013 (nationsreportcard.gov/reading_math_2013).

All schools will eventually encounter challenges or roadblocks in at least one crucial area. A school with high academic achievement may have a demoralized and non-collaborative teaching staff. A school with a respectful and orderly culture may be underperforming in academics or have strained relations with parents and the community. Few schools perform equally well in every regard, and all schools run up against similar problems from time to time.

For example, a majority of U.S. public school students come from low-income families, according to a new analysis of 2013 federal data, a statistic that has profound implications for the nation. The Southern Education Foundation reports that 51 percent of students in prekindergarten through twelfth grade in the 2012–2013 school year were eligible for the federal program that provides free and reduced-price lunches.[2] This troubling situation affects nearly every school district in the country and is an issue that won't be going away anytime soon.

I believe in an approach that I call "visionary school leadership." By that I mean intentional leadership: Everything you do as a school leader must have a clear goal and must be carried out through a systematic, consistent process. Laying out the core principles of visionary leadership, this book will give you specific ways to meet challenges by implementing proven, tested methods that I have successfully used as an administrator in three difficult school environments.

While this book *will* look at theory and data to support school improvement, it is more than a theoretical or data-driven book. It is always practical and concrete. It is designed to help school leaders implement the day-to-day and week-by-week changes that are crucial to improving school performance. Learning can only take place when a school has a culture of respect and harmony. And that kind of culture is not built just on theory or data, but on paying attention to small, tangible details—rules for bathroom use, how trays are emptied in the cafeteria, how students are taught to walk in the hallways, and many other situations. The same detailed, hands-on approach is needed in coaching and developing your professional staff. The ability to initiate difficult conversations with underperforming teachers, to closely observe and monitor their classroom teaching, and to take steps

---

[2] Suitts, Steve. "A Majority Research Bulletin: Low Income Students Now a Majority in the Nation's Public Schools." Southern Education Foundation, 2015 (www.southerneducation.org).

to improve their performance is crucial in improving your school. Theory and data are important, but the key to unlocking their power lies with your ability to effectively implement changes according to what the numbers are telling you.

The lessons and advice I offer were not taught to me in college or graduate school. I learned them on the job. When I first came to a K–8 school as an assistant principal, we didn't have anyone guiding us in how to improve a severely underperforming school. I had taught in the Chicago Public Schools for many years, but Howe School of Excellence was my first experience in a high-stakes, high-pressure administrative setting. Despite my extensive classroom experience, there were many things I didn't know about being an administrator in a struggling school. So the principal and I experimented and tweaked things as we went along. If a strategy worked, we kept it. If not, we went back to the drawing board and tried something new. There was no book or manual to show us the way.

The Hands-On Guide to School Improvement, based on this process of trial and error, seeks to fill that gap. You'll be able to use this book to address your most pressing challenges, from creating a culture of harmony and respect to making instructional leadership the focal point of your daily routine. Whether it's the "small stuff" that matters greatly, or the "big picture" of student achievement, *The Hands-On Guide to School Improvement* provides practical guidance that has been successful in the "real world" of three public schools. It shows you:

- how to create rules and procedures that lead to respect and harmony in classrooms, bathrooms, hallways, and cafeterias.
- how to create and implement consistent and effective disciplinary measures.
- how to spend 70 percent of your time out of the office, monitoring teachers and focusing on instructional leadership.
- how to make ongoing professional development the centerpiece of your work with teachers.
- how to empower teachers to manage their classrooms effectively and deal with difficult issues.
- how to initiate difficult conversations with underperforming or unprofessional teachers, and how to recruit effective teachers.

The book is organized into nine chapters, addressing key challenges you will face as an administrator:

- Twelve Core Principles and Practices of Visionary Leadership
- Developing a Strategic Plan for All Stakeholders
- Evaluating Your School and Staff
- Culture and Climate—Establishing a Positive, Safe, and Nurturing Environment
- Professional Development—Creating and Sustaining a Proficient Learning Community
- The Specifics of Instructional Leadership
- Using Academic Interventions Effectively
- Working with Common Core State Standards
- Building Quality Parent Partnerships

Throughout the book, I rely on real-life examples from my work as an administrator to illustrate key points and practices. You'll find some of these examples in sidebars under the heading "From the Principal's Desk." Sometimes I use the name Great School Academy in place of the real names of schools where I've worked. Similarly, while the stories I tell are true, all teachers' names have been changed. I've also included forms and documents I have used as a hands-on instructional leader, some of which are provided as reproducibles that you can adapt to your own situation and needs. See page vii for instructions for downloading these forms, which you can customize and print out. In addition, a short list of questions follows each chapter, encouraging you to reflect on the material you've read and on your goals as an administrator.

I also regularly refer to Charlotte Danielson's *Enhancing Professional Practice: A Framework for Teaching,* which I have found to be an invaluable guide in my work as an administrator. Danielson's four domains—Planning and Preparation, Classroom Environment, Instruction, and Professional Responsibilities—help frame my standards for teacher excellence.

In the end, no one book can show you the path to successful school reform. I'm not suggesting a one-size-fits-all approach in this book. The schools where I served as an administrator required particular approaches to deal with discipline and academic achievement. Not every school requires exactly the tactics I suggest. Instead, you must test, adapt, and apply your own practices, based on your particular school, teaching staff, and circumstances. *The Hands-On Guide to School Improvement* is designed to help you do that, supplementing and informing your efforts as an administrator.

I invite you to contact me and share your stories or to tell me how the book was useful to you. I applaud your work and wish you success and satisfaction in your endeavors.

Evelyn M. Randle-Robbins, M.A.
help4kids@freespirit.com
c/o Free Spirit Publishing
6325 Sandburg Road, Suite 100
Golden Valley, MN 55427-3674

Everything I recommend in this book has been tried and tested in the day-to-day realities of challenging school environments.

CHAPTER ONE
Twelve Core Principles and Practices of Visionary Leadership

On that March day in 2008, it would be an understatement to say that I was extremely nervous.

Ms. Smith and I were making our first visit to a struggling K–8 school located on Chicago's west side. In September, the two of us—Ms. Smith as the principal and myself as the assistant principal—would be taking over at the school. We were visiting the outgoing principal (whom we would be replacing, along with her entire staff) to get a sense of what we would be facing in the fall.

I had been a classroom teacher since 1992 and was no newcomer to the challenges of underperforming schools. But this was my first assignment as an administrator. Ms. Smith had never been a principal before and I had never been an assistant principal. I had no clue about what it took to transform a school. All I could think about were the previous administrators I had worked for, and how harried and distant they often seemed.

The enormity of the challenge hit me the moment we walked through the school's front doors. The school was in chaos and the noise level was sky-high. Kids who should have been in class were scampering through the halls. Instead of checking us in or welcoming us, the security guard slumped in his chair, as if seeking refuge from the bedlam.

"What's all the noise?" I asked him.

"Oh, that's just lunch," he replied.

As we explored further, we saw that the building was dilapidated. I was struck by the peeling paint, dirty floors, and broken water fountains. I thought to myself: *Is this what we think of our children? Is this how much we value them?*

As Ms. Smith and I peeked into classrooms, we saw no sign of structure or discipline. Teachers and students yelled at each other. Kids sat atop their desks, sometimes pounding on them. In one classroom, a substitute teacher read the newspaper while the entire class was in an uproar. There was no lunchroom. Instead, lunch was being served in shifts in two crowded classrooms.

Had I seen glimpses of schools like this in my career? Yes, I had. But during the previous four years I had been at a much more successful school with a modern interior, up-to-date technology, and a lot of parent participation. When Ms. Smith first contacted me, she asked if I could handle coming to the west side of Chicago, because she knew it would be difficult territory.

When Ms. Smith and I met with the departing principal, she wasn't angry. In fact, she welcomed the coming changes. "This should have been done years ago," she told us. She added, "Don't keep anyone from this staff. They're just not good for students." They had been around for years, she said, and had become complacent.

The principal told us story after story about incompetent teachers—how she had unsuccessfully tried to remove them or take some kind of corrective action. Many were angry and bitter, because now they had to find new jobs by the end of the summer. The principal also showed us knives and other weapons that had been confiscated from students. Many of the school's discipline referrals were for the most aggressive student misconduct.

That day in the school, we could feel the tension around us. Many teachers had mentally checked out already and were just going through the motions, while the students were left to do what they wanted. As we were leaving, we knew we had a huge challenge in front of us. But I didn't feel intimidated by it. Rather, I felt charged. We had a job to do, and I was passionate about getting it done and about fundamentally changing the way those students experienced school. Later that month, Ms. Smith and I began picking a new staff for September.

If you walk into that school today, more than seven years later, you'll see a totally transformed environment. You'll be greeted by a warm staff. You'll see a clean school with creative bulletin boards displaying lots of student work. Students walk the halls quietly, in orderly lines. You'll glance into inviting classrooms and see teachers engaged with their students. Test scores and attendance have risen dramatically, while disciplinary infractions have decreased significantly. And the school now has a real lunchroom.

The difference is between night and day. This book explains how we got there. The core principles I describe will help you:

- create a culture of high-quality learning for students and staff
- develop students who learn more and who can compete academically on standardized assessments
- transform your school into a place where learning is contagious, where kids are eager to come to class and participate, where high achievement is the norm, and where parents and community members become working partners in your success story.

The first core principle in creating and sustaining an effective school is inspiring, supportive, and visionary leadership. Leadership starts from the top; the principal or academic director sets the tone for an entire school. That tone can be negative or it can be positive. I've seen both in my career. In improving school performance, it's absolutely imperative that you provide clear, focused, and intentional leadership. Without such positive leadership, it will be very difficult for you to create transformation.

In the rest of this chapter, I'll explore twelve essential components of effective, visionary leadership. Throughout the book, I'll continually refer back to them and elaborate upon these components.

#1: Speak to Inspire

Inspiring your staff means letting them know that they're the people you want on your team, and that you know they'll help your school overcome whatever obstacles it may face. It means recognizing and empowering that very personal part of them that first drew them to become teachers. They chose the profession for reasons beyond just liking children. They wanted to do something to change society for the better, and they knew that working with students would be the best way to effect that change. Inspiring your staff means speaking to their purpose in life, and acknowledging the reasons why they do what they do. To inspire your staff, work to connect with them and let them know that you realize not everyone can do this work, that they're the right people for the job, and that you're glad to have them on board. A good leader makes teachers feel appreciated.

Start off the year with an inspirational talk with your teachers. Then, throughout the year have one-on-one conversations with them, especially at crucial times. Around testing time, for example, teachers can get frustrated and tired. That's a good time to let your staff know their work isn't in vain and say: "I see everything you're doing, I know you're putting in more than 100 percent, and I appreciate it." Just like anyone else, teachers gain strength and energy from recognition and acknowledgment.

Yes, there are going to be hard days, and things may get more difficult before they get a whole lot better. That's all the more reason to let your staff know that you're on their side and eager to work together. Inspire your staff though little gestures. Cater breakfasts and lunches for them. Give them appreciative cards, plaques, and "hallway high fives." The little things can go a long way toward inspiring your staff.

The first core principle in creating and sustaining an effective school is inspiring, supportive, and visionary leadership.

Too many administrators talk to teachers about what they're doing wrong, but not about what they're doing well. When you begin a conversation with, "I'm so glad you're a part of my staff," you're helping that teacher feel good about being part of your vision. You're empowering that teacher. Sincere praise goes a long way. And when you can walk into classrooms and ask teachers about their weekends or how their parents are doing, it shows that you care about your staff as individuals, not just as employees.

What you do as an administrator affects everyone. Teachers take your positive energy back to their classrooms and transfer it to their students. In turn, students start treating each other better. Inspiration starts at the top and filters all the way down. Tangible progress will result throughout the school year.

#2: Connect Staff with a Vision

To be effective in improving school performance, you need a detailed plan for how you're going to make that happen. In fact, you need multiple plans. There has to be a plan for transforming culture and climate. There has to be a plan for transforming instruction. And there has to be a plan for transforming teaching, or professional development. Change can't be dictated from the top: "I'm the new principal, so everyone follow me." Your staff has to clearly perceive the short-term and long-term goals and benefits of the changes you're working to make.

When you hire and train teachers and staff to begin the process of transforming your school, you need those people to connect with your vision for the school. You have to clearly and passionately articulate that vision so they will say, "Hey, I want to be a part of this thing. It's going to be transformative work and it's going to change—or even save—the lives of students." And you have to not only articulate the vision, but find a way to make it tangible and doable. These steps—which will be described in greater detail later in the book—will help you do this:

• Lead your staff in a creative workshop to develop the mission and vision.
• Create teambuilding activities to strengthen staff cohesion.
• Discuss goal setting with all staff members during one-on-one meetings. Ask: How will their actions contribute to the vision?

A central part of any transformative vision is conveying high expectations. So talk about high expectations at professional development meetings. Devote student assemblies to the subject, especially at the start of the year. Tell students your expectations for them are 200 percent, and make it clear that they must work to meet these expectations. Emphasize these points continually throughout the school year.

Constantly keep your vision front and center in everything you do. Describe it in the simplest possible terms, so people remember it and can carry it forward. At every professional development meeting, reiterate that vision. For example:

• To provide high-quality, standards-based instruction for all students
• To promote the value of learning, emphasizing creativity, character, and social-emotional development
• To nurture quality performance among students and staff, so that everyone is able to reach their highest potential through a differentiated, effective, and rigorous curriculum within a caring, safe, and orderly environment
• To prepare and equip all students to be contributors to a global society

Talk regularly and passionately about how you're going to make these goals become reality. It's okay for a teacher to email you and say, "I have some thoughts about my role as it relates to the vision. Can I bounce some things off you, while you give me more clarity?" In a positive school culture, that kind of collaboration happens all the time. It gives teachers confidence that they can make the vision happen.

#3: Support Your Staff Around the Little Things

Seemingly little things can often disgruntle teachers, especially when they already feel stressed or overwhelmed. Schools located in high-poverty areas, in particular, often don't have the supplies and luxuries that other schools have, and the disbursement of materials and funds may be limited. If teachers can't get a pack of pencils, make copies, or receive supplies from the main office, they may feel angry because of it. In turn, they may struggle to teach effectively. If these things are taking place, supportive leadership is faltering.

To prevent this scenario, you can work on anticipating these "little things" and preventing them to the best of your ability. Buy supplies at the start of the year and provide teachers with pencils, pens, paper, staplers, pencil sharpeners, folders, and crayons—all those things that can make such a huge difference. If your school has uniforms, you can purchase these well before the start of the school year so no one is scrambling at the last minute. You can ensure that necessities such as heating and cooling systems are working in all classrooms. You can also work to be sure that every classroom is set up with minimal technology needs and all teachers have been trained on any new technology before the year begins.

This sends an important message: we're not going to bicker and argue over this stuff. In transforming a school, you've got bigger fish to fry. When children sit down in their seats, their teacher must be ready and able to teach effectively.

#4: Know How to Delegate

In my early days as an administrator, I'd come home overloaded with work. My husband observed, "If you have that much to do, then you haven't delegated." That was a powerful moment of realization. I had hired a highly capable and experienced staff, yet I wasn't empowering them to use their skills to the maximum.

An effective leader has to empower her entire staff and others in the school family—not just teachers, but also parents and caregivers, community members, and partnering organizations. This is a key aspect of improving school performance. At the end of the day, a leader can't do it all herself. You have to communicate the vision and present a coherent plan to achieve that vision. And then you have to send forth your staff to carry it out. That requires delegation.

Be confident in your team members and let them do their jobs. Trust that you've made the right decisions in hiring them or keeping them on your staff. If you're not delegating, you're not using your staff's talents to the fullest.

#5: Create "Buy-In"

Working with adults can sometimes be more difficult than working with students. For the most part, students are going to comply because you have authority over them. You can generally win them over by providing structure, positive support, and social services.

You can't always win over adults this way, however. If you don't connect well with your staff and build a trusting relationship with them, problems will develop, often over the smallest things. That's why many administrators are short, easily frustrated, and not as accessible as you'd like them to be. A huge issue in improving performance is assembling the right people and communicating with them in the right way.

That means creating buy-in—the motivation and desire among teachers and other partners to work with you to fulfill the vision. Buy-in means people agree to support your goals, often by becoming involved in creating those goals. My experiences with administrators over the years—both positive and negative—affect how I run my school today. By doing positive things for staff, you can create buy-in and strengthen their willingness to work hard with you to fulfill your vision. Without that cooperation, no vision can reach fruition. Positive things may include a staff attendance incentive in the form of chocolate bars or other treats, which you can pass out with a note reading, "You're worth a lot to our school. Thank you for

A central part of any transformative vision is conveying high expectations.

being here every day!" Additionally, you could feature a Teacher of the Week in each newsletter, highlighting special events, valuable skills, or notable accomplishments.

At one school where I taught, the principal was very "old school." She would walk into our classrooms in an intimidating manner, sit at our desks while we were teaching, and go through our desks and file drawers (she considered this part of our observation). She also gave us each a piece of hot pink paper with these rules listed on it:

Don't come late.

Don't talk in the halls.

Don't leave the restroom unlocked.

Don't submit your lesson plans late.

She seemed to blame teachers for everything, and everything she said had a negative tone, even her "good morning." Getting a compliment from her was like pulling teeth. She didn't listen to her staff, scheduling morning meetings at 7:45, although none of us wanted to meet that early. Even when she offered to pay us to attend, no one did. She was also completely controlling. Once she walked into a teacher's room and saw something about handwriting instruction she didn't like. She bought every teacher a student-level cursive handwriting book and gave us a due date for completing the assignments. I was stunned and angry. I looked around at the other teachers in the meeting and wanted to say, "Is she serious?"

Not surprisingly, this principal didn't create buy-in. No one would stay after work or take on special projects. As a result, she struggled to increase academic performance. A lot of the staff gave up and just collected their checks.

At another school where I taught, I had the opposite experience: I saw how a truly effective leader creates buy-in. This principal came into my classroom and gave me the constructive feedback I needed. She was warm and supportive. At our Tuesday meetings she complimented the staff, pleasantly and directly. She held teacher appreciation breakfasts and lunches, and gave us small gifts. At the end of the school year she held an ice cream party for the staff, gave a nice going-away talk, and chatted with us about our plans for the summer. At other schools I had worked hard, but at that school I worked *smarter*.

I told myself, "If I become a school principal, I'm going to do that."

When teachers trust you and know that you care about them, you'll get so much more from them. They'll stay longer to make sure projects are taken care of. They'll come in early, because they have a sense of camaraderie. They'll work more collaboratively with you and their teammates. But, for this to happen, they have to feel that you respect them and care about them.

#6: Be Proactive and Take Chances

When transforming a school, you can't wait until every detail is perfectly planned to take action. As an administrator, work to start new programs and to try new ideas proactively, even if you don't know exactly what's going to happen or what the results will be. You'll only see change by making changes, not by waiting until you can be 100 percent sure about every new idea.

If you don't encourage teachers to try new things quickly, they may grow hesitant to do so. This issue arose at one school when we were trying a major change in how teachers worked with students. We wanted to cluster kids in fifth through eighth grades in small groups according to their ability levels, not their grade levels. We discussed this "shift," as we called it, during the fall term, but some staff wanted to postpone trying it until after the winter break. Other staff wanted to start right away and work out the kinks as we went along, so we would know what worked (and didn't work) by the spring term. That's the approach I favored: Let's go ahead and get this done now! Soon everyone was on board, we made the shift, and it was a great success.

I absolutely love that thinking. Try to make it your motto as an administrator: Don't wait to make changes. And when changes don't fit your vision, then you'll know, sooner rather than later, where and how you need to make further changes and adjustments.

#7: Initiate Crucial and Difficult Conversations

An effective leader is able to initiate important conversations with staff—especially when those conversations are difficult. This is essential, especially when you can't replace an entire staff and must bring existing staff up to speed. Being honest with staff about improving their performance is critical to your success. When you're working with employees who are not meeting expectations, you have to be able to say, "What I saw in your classroom wasn't effective. I have a suggestion for trying it a different way." You have to be able to deal with staff directly and say, "I'd like to share something that I believe will enhance your instruction."

When I was a classroom teacher, one of my principals struggled to have critical conversations with her staff around instruction and discipline. The school was surrounded by housing projects, served low-income students, and had its challenging days. Even with these challenges, the school's culture and performance would have improved greatly if the principal had gone into classrooms and initiated difficult conversations with teachers who weren't doing their jobs. Instead, she stayed in her office and staff never saw her.

You'll only see change by making changes.

One reason she had difficulty making her expectations known was that she had gotten too close to her staff and had lost her professional distance. Naturally, it's important to be cordial and friendly with your colleagues. But it's just as important to remember that, first and foremost, you are their administrator and supervisor. Hold your staff accountable, just as you, in turn, will be held accountable by your superiors.

When a staff member is not meeting your expectations, don't postpone starting the tough conversation you need to have. Pull the teacher aside—in private, if possible—and say, "According to what we discussed in our staff handbook about lesson plans, your lesson plans are late," or, "Your lesson plans are not as detailed as I would like them to be. How can I support you around this?"

The teacher may say she had a busy weekend, or may mention another extenuating circumstance, and that's okay. You can allow an occasional excuse, but the teacher has to know by the end of the conversation that you expect detailed lesson plans on your desk before six a.m. on Monday or there will be consequences.

If you don't initiate difficult conversations in a prompt manner, you risk losing control of your staff and perpetuating or exacerbating whatever challenges your school is facing, rather than confronting and overcoming them.

Also remember that *how* you have the conversation is just as important as having it at all. The old saying really does apply: "It's not what you say, but how you say it." Delicate situations will arise and you will have to address them. For example, you might have to tell employees that their attire is not professional enough. You can be effective in communicating your expectations through the way you frame the issue: "We're striving for a professional look in this school. I'm asking you to try a different style of dress." Or you may say to a teacher who struggles with promptness, "Please be here on time. If you are late more than three times, we'll need to have a talk." Whatever topic you need to address, make sure you leave behind your frustration and anger before you speak. You can communicate on a wide range of issues with your staff, if you always remember to communicate in the right way.

Frequent communication creates a stronger bond with your staff and makes it easier to have difficult conversations when needed. For example, in my school I meet with my staff at grade-level meetings once a month, cluster meetings every other Wednesday, and professional development on the other Wednesdays. If you don't interact frequently with your staff, it will be much harder to make your expectations known when a problem does arise.

#8: Pay Attention to Detail

Many schools want to improve their cultures. An effective leader must establish a positive school culture well before the first day of school. To do this, you need to recruit like-minded people to help you build and nurture that culture.

Two insurance salespeople once visited one of my schools and said to me, "We go into a lot of schools, and we've never seen one this quiet. There's a really nice spirit and everyone's so friendly." One way that you can create that type of culture and spirit in your school is by paying attention to details. One of the mottoes around my school is, "Sweat the small stuff." Little things that take place in school, if not addressed, can have large ramifications. Something as seemingly minor as attire can make a surprising difference to the school's atmosphere and even classroom performance. As basketball coach John Wooden said, "It's the little details that are vital. Little things make big things happen."

Sweating the small stuff grows out of your vision for management and organization. It becomes common practice when your staff buys into certain common principles and goals. Sweating the small stuff will mean different things to different people, but for me it means that my school looks neat, there's no litter on the floor or graffiti on the walls (inside or out), and everyone respects the environment.

It also means taking responsibility for everyone's success. When I was a teacher, there were times when I would walk down the hallway and ignore other classes that were misbehaving. But now I tell my staff: "They're not just *your* students, they're *our* students." Think of the message a teacher sends when she leads her class quietly down the hallway but passes a chaotic class without saying anything. It sends a much different message if that teacher stops and says something to the unruly students. By doing this, she both supports her fellow teacher and also sends a clear message to the students about proper behavior.

This may seem like a small thing, but again, you have to sweat the small stuff. If one student is acting inappropriately, the teacher should make sure the student understands the school's expectations, even if the student is in another class. By doing this, the teacher makes clear what's acceptable in the school and what is not. Using this approach and mindset, you'll work toward excellence in everything you do at your school, no matter how small. When the small things are done well, big things will follow.

 FROM THE PRINCIPAL'S DESK

At my school, one way we sweat the small stuff is practicing something called "Do It Again." For example, we have a zero noise level rule. Students are expected to pass quietly through the hallways at all times. If students are noisy and unorganized lining up for restroom break, the teacher will say, "I like the way some of you did that, but I know we can do it better. Everybody sit back down because we're going to **do it again.**"

This technique comes from Doug Lemov's book *Teach Like a Champion*.[3] Lemov focuses on setting and maintaining high behavioral expectations in the classroom. He explains that the Do It Again technique is effective for many reasons, but, most importantly, because it ends with success. It helps students build the habit of doing routines right, again and again.

---

[3] This material is reproduced with permission of John Wiley & Sons, Inc.

#9: Model Positive Behavior

To help establish a positive tone and atmosphere, establish what you want to see from your staff, and then become a model of that behavior. Make your expectations tangible by showing them. Your staff will do what they see their leader doing. (Or, as Oprah has said, "You teach people how to treat you.") This means letting people know what works for you as the school leader and what doesn't work. For instance, you can say, "I expect meetings to be run a certain way." Then follow up on what you've said by modeling, step-by-step, how you want meetings to be run and make sure that everyone understands your expectations.

In addition to modeling proper procedures and techniques, you—as an effective instructional leader—are also modeling a way of interacting with others. Modeling expectations covers a wide range of behaviors, from being prompt at staff meetings to the way teachers speak to students. And when you demonstrate those expectations through your own actions, you are setting an example not only for staff, but also for students. The things you and your teachers say are important, but students also watch and learn from the things you do. In transforming a school, you need to instill respect, positivity, and cooperation as norms. So it's important to also look for these qualities when hiring your staff. If you interview a teacher or observe him doing a demo lesson and get the sense that he isn't a pleasant or respectful person, then he isn't going to be your first choice as a new hire.

Meanwhile, continue to model pleasant behavior for both teachers and students, even when it's tough. Yes, I do have days when I want to jump on my desk, pull out my hair, and scream. But I sure don't want to see that behavior in my classrooms. Always be aware of how you conduct yourself and how it affects your school's culture.

#10: Be Visible and Hands-On

I know firsthand that administrators can easily get caught up in phone calls and paperwork. But to make big changes at your school, you have to come out of the main office. If you become a hostage to your desk, your teachers will not feel supported. And if they don't feel supported, they'll probably start having conversations with each other that will not help you reach your goals:

"I like teaching, and I love my kids, but I'm not sure I want to stay here because no one is steering the ship."

"I never see my principal. She never comes in here!"

"I want to be in a school where the principal offers me guidance."

To prevent these murmurs and grumbles, be visible. Show your staff that you're hands-on in running the school. Be clear with teachers about what's taking place, both inside and outside the classroom. Are you going to be a manager who deals strictly with operations? Or are you going to be an instructional leader?

An effective principal is skilled in both roles, but I spend most of my day in classrooms, observing teachers, and providing instructional feedback and coaching. If you're not a hands-on administrator, closely monitoring teachers and making suggestions on how they can improve their craft, you will struggle to lift student achievement or make the other changes you want to see.

#11: Market Your School

Being willing and able to "market" your school means having the ability to share what is happening at your school with businesses and outside partnerships—who in turn may have the ability (and willingness) to provide assistance and support the school may need.

Part of this marketing is how you present your school building itself. If visitors come to your building, will they see wonderful examples of student work on your walls? Will they see posters describing what your school is about? You can use these types of visual representations to draw in families to your school and feel engaged and supportive of your mission. After all, you *want* to draw people to your school in a positive way. You want to be on the news for something fantastic happening in your school. You want parents saying wonderful things about your school, and hearing their students say, "I love going to school." It's all a matter of promoting the wonderful things that happen in your school. It's easy to find things that aren't so wonderful, but good things are happening in your school, and you need to find a way to put that message out there.

To do this, you don't need to spend a lot of time and money promoting your school. Type up your achievements on some glossy paper and hand them out at report card pickup, back-to-school events, and so on. Hold events like open houses and ice cream socials, inviting parents and other community members into your building. Blog about your school and the great things you're doing. Post on Twitter, Facebook, Pinterest, and Instagram to share news and anecdotes. See if your school can be featured in a local newspaper, weekly magazine, or other medium.

If you connect with the community and put a face on what you're doing and highlight your achievements, you can get a lot of support. For instance, you may form community partnerships that can provide you with school supplies and other materials, as well as moral support (and perhaps even positive publicity) for your mission. By marketing your school, you may also attract parents whose students are working above grade level. And that is going to add to your ability to improve academic performance—which in turn will give you something positive you can use in marketing your school!

#12: Set Up Small Victories and Quick Wins

Small victories and quick wins at the start of the school year help your staff bond with your vision and believe in its possibility. One way to do this is to establish monthly incentives for staff around their attendance, as well as around student attendance. It's a small step to arrange for those incentives, but they will help you build a culture of excellence.

Another way to set up small victories is by reaching out to the community at the start of the school year. Conduct a community canvas by walking around the area and introducing yourself and your staff to your neighbors and your community members—the people you are there to serve. Try to include your entire staff, not just teachers but also teacher assistants, bus monitors, and lunchroom staff. And as part of this day of outreach, have a back-to-school barbecue. Invite everyone, not just parents with schoolchildren.

You and your staff may be pleasantly surprised by how open and receptive your community is to your efforts and engagement. You might hear people say things like, "Wow, it's so cool that you guys took the time to come by my house and introduce yourselves!"

This is the type of "quick win" that will help your teachers stay motivated and charged up to reach your school's goals. It's also a victory for your community members, who will see that they have a team of committed, passionate educators in their midst, and that your school is an asset to the neighborhood. Improving school performance can be a long journey, but setting yourself up for these successes will help you and your team see the light at the end of the tunnel.

FROM THE PRINCIPAL'S DESK

When I did my first community canvas and barbecue, a lot of my teachers and staff members were skeptical. In the past, they had been reluctant to interact with the neighborhood. But having done community outreach before I was confident it would yield good results.

On the Saturday we held the barbecue, the schoolyard was flooded with people. We talked with the neighbors about the community. We discussed students' needs. We talked about what we wanted to accomplish that school year and the programs we had in mind.

The teachers bonded with the community. They were able to talk and establish a sense of collaboration. Call it a small victory or a big one, but it was a victory. My teachers went away thinking, "I can succeed because I have community support. I can work with this community."

Room for Reflection

VISIONARY LEADERSHIP

- What is your leadership style? How would you describe it?

- After reading this chapter, what thoughts do you have about changing your leadership style? What areas of leadership do you need to improve?

- Pick one leadership skill discussed in this chapter. How would you change or develop your approach to using that skill?

- What are some ways you can create more buy-in among your staff members?

- What more can you do to market your school and connect with your community?

CHAPTER TWO
Developing a Strategic Plan for All Stakeholders

A key component in school improvement is having a detailed strategic plan for the school year. Whether you're a new administrator or a returning one, you may face high expectations for changing the ways things are and instilling new standards for school culture, discipline, and achievement. Multiple constituencies are watching your performance, and without a clearly defined plan that takes into account their main needs and desires, it will be difficult to accomplish the changes you are seeking.

In the weeks before school starts, identify your core constituencies, the objectives you want to achieve with each one, and a detailed plan for achieving each of those objectives. In my work as a principal, I've identified the following four core constituencies that need to be brought on board: Teachers and staff; students; parents and caregivers; and community members.

As an instructional leader, part of your job is to understand the different perspectives of each group and to build effective relationships with them that support your mutual efforts to improve school performance. Then, for each group, you will need to establish key objectives to be achieved. In this chapter, I'll lay out a detailed example of what your objectives might be and the strategic plans you could follow to reach those objectives.

Objectives by Constituency Group

CONSTITUENCY 1: TEACHERS AND STAFF
Objective: Establish team-oriented working relationships based on mutual respect and collaboration to further enhance the quality of education provided to all students.

CONSTITUENCY 2: STUDENTS

Objective: Create positive avenues of communication between the administrative team and students in order to create a learning environment that is challenging yet supportive.

CONSTITUENCY 3: PARENTS AND CAREGIVERS

Objective: Cultivate strong and effective relationships so that parents feel welcomed and valued in the education of their students, and seek ways in which their advocacy and contributions can benefit all students.

CONSTITUENCY 4: COMMUNITY MEMBERS

Objective: Establish open communication that allows for community members to share their aspirations for our students, their concerns about educational programs, and ways in which they can contribute to our mission to educate and inspire every student.

PUTTING IT ALL TOGETHER

Once you've established core objectives for each constituency, the next step is to develop a detailed strategic plan that describes the action steps you and your team will take before school starts, at the start of the school year, and throughout the following months to reach your objectives.

The remainder of this chapter outlines a three-phase plan that you can use to conduct and implement strategic planning with your core constituencies, both before school starts and throughout the school year.

Strategic Plan, Phase One: Before School Starts (May to August)

CONSTITUENCY 1: TEACHERS AND STAFF

Objectives:
- Learn more about members of the school family and build positive relationships to ensure a smooth transition.
- Develop and cement a culture of open dialogue and communication surrounding ideas, goals, and personal values related to education.

- Establish a team-oriented professional learning community focused on collaboration and enthusiasm.
- Learn more about what drives the success of the school in order to build on that success.
- Ensure academic achievement and growth for all students.
- Determine priorities for the school based on current school data and design a plan of action focusing on these priorities.

ACTIONS TO TAKE BEFORE SCHOOL STARTS

Email or mail introductory letter to all teachers and staff. This letter should go out to every member of the school staff, from the custodial staff all the way up to teachers at your highest grade level. In it, introduce yourself, citing your experiences, values, beliefs, and your passion for creating high-achievement success for students. Also share some of what you want to see as the end result in school performance. This allows the staff to get a sense on paper of what kind of person you are, your qualifications, and your core beliefs. However, do not, at this point, go into great detail about your school improvement plans. You can communicate that information later in the year. See Figure 1 on the next page for a sample letter.

Invite staff to a "Meet the Principal" social. Schedule a short social event to meet your staff and introduce yourself to them. This will not be an information-gathering session as described in the next chapter, but rather an informal event where you can begin the process of getting to know one another in a social setting.

Survey staff on school climate, professional development, and schedules. Develop a survey that can be emailed to all staff members to ascertain their views on school climate, professional development, school safety, parent relations, and other areas that are important to you. (For a sample survey, see the reproducible on pages 37–39.) This information will be used to implement a comprehensive professional development plan throughout the school year. I'll discuss professional development (PD) in more detail in Chapters Five and Six.

Review schedules and staff handbook. Familiarize yourself with these important documents, noting ways they can be changed and improved.

FIGURE 1: **SAMPLE INTRODUCTORY LETTER TO STAFF**

Dear Great School Academy Staff,

With great excitement, I write you my first staff letter of the year. The summer has passed quickly, but it has been filled with meeting people and learning more about our wonderful school. Great School Academy has a wealth of knowledge among its staff members. It's also family-oriented and collaboratively committed to putting students first. Without a doubt, I am proud to be the principal and instructional leader of Great School Academy.

As you await the beginning of the school year, I ask that you keep our new district initiatives in mind:

What We Teach
Common Core State Standards that outline a higher bar for what our students need to know in order for them to succeed in college and careers.

How We Teach
A new, comprehensive teacher evaluation system, designed to provide teachers with tools and support to improve their practice and better drive student learning.

Time to Teach
The Full School Day, which will expand instructional time so that our students will have more time on task in reading, math, history, and science. In addition, this change provides time for a real recess so students can exercise and refresh.

I want to recognize all of you for the enthusiasm and caring spirit that you bring to Great School Academy every day. Our most recent data suggests that, along with those attributes, we'll need to continue to commit ourselves to instructional urgency!

Subject	2013–2014	2014–2015	Change
Reading	51.1%	48.4%	Down 2.7%
Math	57.2%	58.1%	Up 0.9%
Science	44.8%	43.9%	Down 0.9%
Composite	52.9%	51.9%	Down 1.0%

Our data clearly calls for us to give 100 percent more. When we maximize instructional time, teach with rigor, make data-driven decisions, and hold ourselves accountable for positive results . . . WE CAN DO ANYTHING!

"Optimism is the faith that leads to achievement; nothing can be done without hope and confidence."
—Helen Keller

Opening Day for all staff is Monday, August 8. A "Welcome Back Breakfast" will take place from 7:50–8:15 a.m. in the school cafeteria to give us the opportunity to say hello to one another. Our Common Core professional development will begin at 8:25 a.m. in the media center. I look forward to seeing you again and beginning our journey of helping our students become the best they can be.

Please enjoy the remainder of the summer. Take time to pause, reflect, rekindle, renew, create memories, and celebrate life.

Form your Instructional Leadership Team (ILT). Your Instructional Leadership Team, the formation of which is described in detail in Chapter Six, should be developed before the school term starts or shortly thereafter.

Schedule meetings with the ILT to review all key documents, such as mission and vision statements, school progress reports, assessment data, safety and security plans, schedules, attendance data, discipline data, the student handbook, the faculty handbook, parent survey results, and any other information relevant to school performance.

Create a professional development plan and establish an ongoing professional development calendar. This plan will flow from your staff interviews and survey, discussed in detail in Chapter Three. Before school starts, take the following steps to create your PD plan:

- Meet with your ILT to create a PD schedule based on the results of the teacher survey.
- Identify summer PD opportunities.
- Create PD binders for staff that will include agendas, handouts, notes, etc.
- Conduct a PD institute for teachers in September, including an introduction to the Danielson framework for teaching and a team-building day.
- Conduct classroom environment walkthroughs. Visit each classroom before school starts to make sure the environment is clean, orderly, professional, supportive of learning, inviting, and suited to students' needs. (Read more about this in Chapter Four.)

CONSTITUENCY 2: STUDENTS

Objectives:
- Learn more about the students and the challenges they face.
- Create positive avenues of communication between the administration and students, creating a challenging yet supportive learning environment.

ACTIONS TO TAKE BEFORE SCHOOL STARTS

Prepare an interview for student leaders/student council. Student leaders can become valuable partners as you work to improve and transform your school. Ask what they like about your school—and what they think could be even better. They'll appreciate having their voices heard, and you'll learn a lot about where these prominent students are coming from and what they see as important.

Prepare survey for the entire student body. Draft a survey getting a sense of the wider student body's opinions. Ask about students' hopes, concerns, and goals for the year. If possible, have several teachers—and even some former students—review the survey and make suggestions for improvements. Ideally, you would also create a few versions of the survey for different groups or grade levels.

Through these interviews and surveys, which will be conducted after school starts (see page 31 for more discussion), you'll gain valuable information about student attitudes that will inform your decision-making process.

CONSTITUENCY 3: PARENTS AND CAREGIVERS
Objectives:
Cultivate strong and effective relationships so that parents feel welcomed and valued in the education of their students, and seek ways in which their advocacy and contributions can benefit all students.

ACTIONS TO TAKE BEFORE SCHOOL STARTS
Send an introductory letter to parents and caregivers. Write to all parents, introducing yourself and your goals for the coming year. This will help the families of your students feel involved and excited before students even walk in the door for the first day of school. See Figure 2 on page 28 for an example.

Survey parents on their satisfaction and ideas for involvement and participation. This can be done before school via letter or email, or sent home as a "backpack mailing" with students as soon as school starts. The more you know about parents' attitudes, the more success you will have in gaining their involvement.

Schedule weekly "coffee and conversation" chats with parents during the summer. This will keep you apprised of any issues needing your attention and will enable you to keep parents informed of your plans and progress.

Update families on progress of your findings and plan of action. Inform parents of your action plan based on surveys of staff, parents, and students.

FIGURE 2: SAMPLE INTRODUCTORY LETTER TO PARENTS AND CAREGIVERS

Dear Great School Academy Family,

I hope you are enjoying your summer and finding ways to rest and relax! Last year, many of us worked together during parent and teacher meetings to identify our priorities for this school year. As a result, we are going to have an exceptional year at Great School Academy.

We will focus on maintaining a safe and orderly environment in our school, providing intervention and enrichment experiences for our children and engaging them in complex reading and writing tasks that will prepare them to enter the best high schools and colleges of their choice. Our teachers will be coming back to school early to begin their professional development, focusing on instructional approaches that will inspire students to value learning, think and respond critically and creatively, and develop innovative ideas and solutions.

I will continue to host monthly parent meetings this year. Our initial sessions will focus on our school priorities and building parent involvement through our Parent Advisory Councils (PAC) and our new Parents on Patrol (POP) program. This year we will also offer more workshops for families, which will help you become better informed about our literacy, math, and science curriculum and ways that you can support children at home. To begin, I am asking that you be prepared to partner with us in increasing the academic progress of your child by doing *at least* the following:

1. Monitor your child's reading and homework assignments. Depending on your child's age, he or she will be expected to read and complete between fifteen and ninety minutes of homework each weekday.

2. Attend a quarterly conference to discuss your child's progress and performance with his or her teachers.

3. Attend school on time. All students should be on the school grounds by 8:00 a.m.

4. Reinforce Great School Academy's expectation that your child comes to school each day ready to follow the rules, listen to adults, and be a productive citizen in our teaching and learning community.

The first day of school is Monday, August 26.

We have a lot to be excited about as we continue our journey to overcome challenges and achieve education excellence. Our library/media center is almost finished, new computers are on the way, and we have an updated school website. **Most importantly, we are committed to improving our teaching and learning approaches so that each student entrusted to our care will demonstrate dramatic gains in achievement this year.**

Join me for our Back to School Event on **Saturday, August 24,** from 11:00 a.m. to 2:00 p.m. All registered students will receive a free book bag with school supplies. There will be food, games, music, and lots of fun.

I hope to see you soon!

Collaborate with parents on Open Houses, Parent Nights, and Curriculum Nights. In your parent survey, solicit feedback on how to best organize, schedule, and conduct these events. The Open House should be held at the school immediately after the school term begins. Discuss your plans for culture and climate, teacher training, and academic achievement. Parent Nights and Curriculum Nights can be held at regular intervals throughout the school year.

CONSTITUENCY 4: COMMUNITY MEMBERS
Objectives:
Establish communication with community members so they can share their aspirations for your students, their concerns about your educational programs, and ways in which they can contribute to your mission.

ACTIONS TO TAKE BEFORE SCHOOL STARTS
Send an introductory letter to community leaders and organizations. Like the letter you send to staff and to parents, this will remind community members of the valuable work being done at your school and will encourage them to be a part of your school's mission.

Schedule a "Meet the Principal" luncheon for leaders of community organizations. Identify key community organizations and meet with them to inform them of your plans for school improvement—as well as community involvement—and to find ways you can work toward mutual collaboration and support.

Strategic Plan, Phase Two: Start of the School Year (August/September)

GENERAL OBJECTIVES
- Prepare for a start to the school year that is focused and intentional.
- Continue to make connections with all stakeholders.
- Determine what steps are necessary for your school to fulfill its vision and mission.
- Determine what your school's educational program needs to look like in order to fulfill your vision and mission.

- Determine "where we are and where we need to go" in order to ensure that you are meeting the educational needs of every student.
- Establish professional relationships that encourage "courageous conversations."

Since the beginning of the school year can be a particularly hectic time, you may want to create a list of tasks that absolutely need to be accomplished in preparation for reaching these objectives. This list can be shared with the administrative team, and you may decide to delegate some of the tasks. The list might look something like this:

1. Review all staff schedules and make revisions if necessary.
2. Create a calendar of school events. Post it on bulletin boards within the building, as well as on your school's website and Facebook page.
3. Create an assessment calendar.
4. Review entry and dismissal procedures.
5. Ensure that all forms and parent handouts are ready for the first day of school.
6. Write the first weekly parent newsletter.
7. Review and update the school website to further strengthen connections between home and school.
8. Create a school public relations folder for distribution to prospective parents and visitors.
9. Review budget and internal accounts.
10. Ensure that all positions are filled, or post e-bulletin announcements if additional new staff is still needed.
11. Make necessary purchases.
12. Create and communicate a schoolwide theme for the year.

CONSTITUENCY 1: TEACHERS
ACTIONS TO TAKE AS SCHOOL STARTS
Schedule one-on-one meetings with each staff member. Use this meeting to learn more about your staff's perspectives about the school and to understand relationships among the staff, using guided questions to gather this information. (This meeting, which is crucial in learning about the strengths and weaknesses of your staff, will be discussed in detail in the next chapter, along with examples of questions to use.)

Set priorities after initial phase of listening and learning, and update staff on your findings. Based on your individual interviews with staff, you will establish priorities for the school year that will be clearly communicated to staff through your strategic plan.

Keep the lines of communication open. Send your staff weekly newsletters. In addition, post your strategic plan in a prominent location in the front office. Regular and open communication is crucial to improving school performance. Be completely transparent with teachers and staff about the challenges you face, the solutions you propose, and the changes you intend to make.

In conjunction with your ILT, determine schoolwide goals. These goals should include items such as the percentage of students to exceed standards, attendance goals for students and teachers, and numbers of student misconduct referrals, along with any other targets important to your mission.

Prepare PD based on Common Core or other state standards for the school year. What do you want to focus on in this year's professional development? What groundwork should you lay before the start of the school year to prepare for a successful PD program?

Choose the first book for study with staff in PD. Identify the first book you'll study with your staff in professional development, based on your top-priority goals and the urgency of your school's needs.

Communicate the schoolwide focus for your first PD meeting. For instance, you might choose to focus your first meeting on Charlotte Danielson's Domain 3b: Using Questioning and Discussion Techniques. Let staff know that this will be the topic of discussion, and, if needed, provide them with references so they can familiarize themselves with key ideas before the meeting.

CONSTITUENCY 2: STUDENTS
ACTIONS TO TAKE AS SCHOOL STARTS
Meet with the student council and other student leaders. Holding a short interview with these key students can reveal much about the student body's prior experiences with the school, their expectations and hopes for change, and the best ways to achieve that change. Having a clear understanding of

students' needs, desires, and past frustrations, as well as their successes, is a key component of improving academic performance.

Having a clear understanding of students' needs, desires, and past frustrations, as well as their successes, is a key component of improving academic performance.

Survey the student body. In addition to your interviews with student leaders, have teachers conduct a short survey of student attitudes, their likes and dislikes, across all grade levels. This can be done shortly after school starts, either as an in-class activity or a homework assignment.

Schedule a "Meet the Principal" ice cream social for students. Schedule a short social event in which you meet the students by grade level or cluster.

Hold assemblies by grade level during the first week of school. Use these assemblies to introduce yourself again, to discuss your goals for academic achievement, and to communicate standards for culture and discipline.

Be visible at entry, dismissal, and lunch periods. As a hands-on leader, you will always be visible, but make sure to be especially visible during the first week of school.

Analyze student surveys. Identify a few key findings from the surveys and discuss these with staff. If appropriate, you can also follow up on these findings with the student body, through assemblies, newsletters, or other channels.

Establish "Student of the Month" luncheons with the principal. Student of the Month luncheons (or breakfasts) are a great way to acknowledge the work of both students and parents. Teachers can select students based on factors such as monthly attendance, consistent adherence to the uniform policy (if applicable), academics, and behavior. Students might receive special certificates, while parents are thanked and encouraged to keep up the great work of supporting their children. It's also a nice touch to take photos of students and parents with the principal, and display these photos in the building or on the school website.

Have a student journalist conduct a "Meet Your Principal" interview. Share this interview in your school newspaper or newsletter to help students get a better sense of their school's leadership.

CONSTITUENCY 3: PARENTS AND CAREGIVERS

ACTIONS TO TAKE AS SCHOOL STARTS

Schedule a "Meet the Principal" luncheon. Schedule a social event to meet parents and introduce your goals for the school.

Schedule monthly focus groups with parents after school starts to address larger topics. Hold these meetings to address important issues that surface during the school year.

Collaborate on Open Houses, Parent Nights, and Curriculum Nights. These are opportunities to share with parents and caregivers what happens at your school on a day-to-day basis. Spend time informing parents of new curriculums and ways to support their children at home. Also give parents opportunities multiple times during the year—not only at report card pickup or parent-teacher conferences—to view their children's classrooms and build great parent-teacher relationships.

Interview parent representatives from across the school. Share the findings from these interviews with staff and use them as a springboard for discussing how you can build on your strengths and address areas of weakness.

CONSTITUENCY 4: COMMUNITY MEMBERS

ACTIONS TO TAKE AS SCHOOL STARTS

Schedule monthly focus groups during the school year to address school issues and community involvement. Brainstorm ways to engage community members—including parents, but also beyond—in conversation about your school as a part of the neighborhood. You can't realistically have one-on-one meetings with everyone in your community, but you do want to create some type of forum where you can share with them your beliefs, values, and goals. By meeting with parents and community resources, you can also listen to their concerns and build relationships. For instance, you could create monthly "Chat-and-Chew" events, at which you provide snacks and mediate discussion about designated topics related to the school's place in the community. You can also hold a quarterly State of the School Address to which you invite parents and other community members. Or, consider inviting members of your local police department to share information— from concerns to progress—about the neighborhood. These kinds of events show the community that your school is being proactive and responsive to the needs of the area it serves.

Attend police district meetings, participate in special functions, and host civic and community organizations. In addition to opening your school's doors to the community, also get out into the community yourself, and encourage your staff to do the same. Attending local meetings and events will allow you and your teachers to get to know your school's neighbors, as well as the leaders of different local organizations. As follow-up activities, some of these organizations' members can become student mentors or speakers for Career Day.

Strategic Plan, Phase Three: Throughout the School Year

As the school year goes on, be sure not to lose focus on your mission. Continue to set clear objectives and goals, such as the following, and keep your core constituencies in the loop about your progress toward these goals.

GOAL 1: COMPLETE UNMET GOALS FROM FIRST THIRTY DAYS OF SCHOOL

- What successes have been achieved in meeting the goals you've established? Identify successful programs, strategies, and interventions that are contributing to a culture of success.
- What are the areas of weakness within your school? Identify those programs, strategies, and interventions that may not be effective.
- Complete a needs assessment with your ILT. A needs assessment can be specific to any area of the school (for instance, discipline, curriculum, or attendance). It allows the Instructional Leadership Team to view data on current systems, practices, and partnerships to decide whether changes are necessary. Every needs assessment should conclude with an action plan of next steps.

GOAL 2: DRIVE FOR RESULTS

Keep staff motivated by clearly articulating your goals. One approach you might use is to create objectives based on Charlotte Danielson's four domains, as shown in the following example.

DOMAIN 1: PLANNING AND PREPARATION

- Create a schedule for weekly lesson plan submissions.
- Create a lesson plan feedback form.
- Work with staff on quarterly goal planning and unit goal planning.

DOMAIN 2: THE CLASSROOM ENVIRONMENT

- Work with teachers to develop behavior management plans that foster positive student behavior. (See Chapter Four for more information on this topic.)
- Implement a model for recognizing and rewarding positive student behavior.
- Implement Student of the Month celebrations.

DOMAIN 3: INSTRUCTION

- Begin weekly or biweekly ILT meetings.
- Notify staff of walkthrough expectations for instruction (student-friendly objectives, visible lesson plans, timely feedback, etc.).
- Conduct initial walkthroughs with ILT for calibration of focus and analysis.
- Conduct regular learning walkthroughs targeting specific areas regarding teaching and learning.
- Implement a Strategy of the Month discussion to dig into specific strategies. You could choose the highlighted strategies from books such as Doug Lemov's *Teach Like a Champion*.
- Hold Wednesday walkthroughs to focus only on questioning and discussion techniques (to implement schoolwide focus).
- Create a formal fall and spring observation schedule and share it with staff.
- Convene weekly ILT meetings to discuss teaching and learning, with the goal of making needed adjustments to instruction as soon as possible.

DOMAIN 4: PROFESSIONAL RESPONSIBILITIES

- Conduct weekly checks of teachers' grade books.
- Encourage teachers to create monthly class newsletters to nurture stronger home-school connections.

- Have staff identify professional goals for the school year. (For example, a target percentage of students exceeding standards, implementing small-group work effectively, working on National Board Certification, and so forth.)
- Implement collegial visits to foster collaboration and professional growth.

Room for Reflection

DEVELOPING A STRATEGIC PLAN

- What aspects of this chapter stood out most for you? Why?
- After reading this chapter, what ideas or approaches will you use to develop a strategic plan for your school?
- Pick one goal discussed in this chapter. How would you change or develop your approach to achieve this goal in your school?
- What plans will you implement to cultivate adult professional learning at your school?

STAFF AND TEACHER SURVEY

This year our school is creating a new School Improvement Plan and we would like your input! Please take a few minutes to think about your experiences and write down your responses to the following questions. Your comments will help direct our improvement efforts to the areas that need it most.

What is your position?
☐ Classroom Teacher   ☐ Teacher Assistant   ☐ School Support Staff
☐ Other (please specify) _____

How long have you worked in the field of education?
☐ Less than 1 year   ☐ 1–2 years   ☐ 3–5 years   ☐ 6–9 years   ☐ 10+ years

What grades do you work with?
☐ Grades 1–3   ☐ Grades 4–6   ☐ Grades 7–8   ☐ Grades 9–12

Based on your personal experience/perspective, indicate yes or no by checking ONE response for each of the following statements.

Can you state our schoolwide mission and vision?   ☐ Yes   ☐ No

What are some ideas for further clarifying and strengthening our mission and vision?

_____

_____

Do you feel that all staff members are invited to contribute to the decision-making process at our school?   ☐ Yes   ☐ No

Is professional development effective at our school?   ☐ Yes   ☐ No

Why or why not? _____

_____

Would you like more instructional support?   ☐ Yes   ☐ No

Why or why not? _____

_____

If yes, in what area(s)? _____

_____

Do you feel valued and appreciated?   ☐ Yes   ☐ No

Why or why not? _____

_____

Do you feel supported by your colleagues?   ☐ Yes   ☐ No

Why or why not? _____

_____

Do you feel supported by the administration?   ☐ Yes   ☐ No

Why or why not? _____

_____

Do you feel our school is safe for staff and students?   ☐ Yes   ☐ No

How could we improve in the area of safety and security?

_____

_____

_____

_____

_____

What kind of expectations do you feel our school has for students, staff, and families?
☐ 1 - very low   ☐ 2 - low   ☐ 3 - average   ☐ 4 - high   ☐ 5 - very high

Does our school have a welcoming atmosphere?   ☐ Yes   ☐ No

Why or why not? _____

_____

Are the school environment and interactions respectful and courteous?   ☐ Yes   ☐ No

Why or why not? _____

_____

What suggestions do you have for improvements to our school environment and culture?

_____

_____

_____

Have you reached out to families to increase their involvement in the school? ☐ Yes ☐ No

Why or why not? _____

_____

_____

If yes, in what way(s)? _____

_____

_____

What suggestions do you have for additional ways our school could connect with families?

_____

_____

_____

_____

_____

_____

_____

What other suggestions do you have for improvements to our school?

_____

_____

_____

_____

_____

_____

_____

_____

Additional comments:

_____

_____

_____

_____

_____

_____

Thank you!

CHAPTER THREE
Evaluating Your School and Staff

A key challenge in improving school performance is evaluating your existing staff by getting a sense of their morale, cohesiveness, and working relations. Whether you're a new administrator or a returning one, you won't necessarily be able to hire a whole new staff as a way of achieving your goals. Instead, you have to assess where your current teachers and staff are and determine how to use their strengths and address their weaknesses. Even if you plan to make major changes in staff, they may need to wait. In the meantime, you need to work with what you've got.

This can present a dilemma. It's essential to assess your staff, and possibly replace some of them. Yet a number of them could be crucial to the school in the short term. For example, Ms. Clark might not be a stellar teacher, but she may be an important leader among your faculty. You need her as your ally for the time being. If you do need to replace her, it will take at least a year. What do you do in the meantime? To use an analogy, a ship's captain cannot make the right choices about her eventual route and destination without first taking careful stock of her crew. In this chapter, I'll discuss the ways you can evaluate your current staff, focus on key qualities, and make decisions about new hires.

Create an Information-Gathering Plan

Regardless of whether you're working to strengthen and reshape an existing staff, hire a lot of new teachers, or do something in between, it's key to know as much as you can about your school and the members of your current team. You can address this need by creating a clear, concrete, and intentional information-gathering plan and putting it into action during the first three to four weeks of school. Through this plan, you will get to know your current staff better, and at the same time shape their first impressions of you.

This plan will allow you to:

- answer staff's questions about the new changes being implemented
- get to know your staff in person, one-on-one
- begin to collectively inspire your staff and lead them in the direction you want to go

Through information gathering, you can design and develop an in-depth professional development (PD) plan to be implemented at the start of the school year. Not everyone can use time during the summer for professional development, but you can formulate a thirty- to ninety-day PD plan that will begin immediately after the school year starts. (Chapter Five addresses professional development in depth.) The first step, though, is to evaluate your staff through one-on-one interviews.

Following are the basic steps of that information-gathering process.

SCHEDULE INTERVIEWS

Begin scheduling one-on-one interviews with the existing staff to get a feel for who you're working with, how they see the school, and what needs to be addressed or changed. The goal is to find out what *their* priorities are before you share your priorities with them.

Scheduling interviews can be tricky, because you may not have a lot of time. You'll want to conduct thirty-minute interviews, so you'll probably have to get creative with people's schedules. In order to accommodate everyone, you may have to give up some weekends or come in early or stay late. It is imperative to meet with everyone. If you fail to do so, that's likely to become a conversation you don't want to hear around the school: "Why didn't she meet with me?"

USE GUIDING QUESTIONS

Ask everyone to bring résumés to their thirty-minute interviews, where you will ask several guiding questions. Sample questions are provided as a reproducible on pages 55–56. Your questions can vary from those suggestions, but they should be designed to collect crucial information about the staff and school.

As you design your questions, think about what you can learn not only about the person you're interviewing but also about how he sees his colleagues. For example, consider the questions, "Which of your colleagues most inspires you? Who can you count on when you need to get something done? Which teachers do you see as school leaders?" A teacher's answers to these queries will tell you who the leaders are in the school and who you need to align yourself with. Whether these are the best teachers or not, you'll want to have these people on your side because of the effect they have on other staff.

Take notes as you interview each staff member. Pay attention to the choice of words and body language as the person responds. Notice what the individual *doesn't* say, as well as what topics seem to elicit strong emotional responses. Do any "hot buttons" get pressed? This will enable you to find out each staff member's passion. A teacher who is very passionate about reading may make the remark that the literacy committee is not working effectively. This is the person you might want on your new literacy committee.

At this point, your evaluation of staff has nothing to do with who has the best math scores or who needs help teaching language arts. Instead, the focus is on learning more about who you're working with, and who's going to be in front of students.

These conversations will help you strengthen relationships, collect data about the school, identify teacher leaders, focus on areas of concern, and establish a few quick wins. If the problem of staff attendance comes up, what can you do right off the bat to address it? Look for ways to inspire the staff that can be implemented quickly, such as rewarding target attendance with gift cards, teacher polo shirts, plaques or trophies, special parking spaces, or schoolwide recognition. Longer-term challenges that emerge from these meetings will be dealt with in turn. But first you want to get some short-term victories under your belt.

HOLD A STAFF SOCIAL

After the meeting send a personal thank-you note to each staff member, along with an invitation to a staff social. It doesn't have to be an elaborate or expensive event. It can be as simple as offering coffee and pastries, something short and sweet that doesn't take too much time and allows you to observe your staff. Once again, let people know who you are and acknowledge that you've met with everyone and enjoyed the conversations.

At this gathering you'll pay attention to group dynamics, alliances, and particular attitudes—who's talking with whom, body language, and facial expressions. Record your impressions after the event.

CONDUCT A PROFESSIONAL DEVELOPMENT SURVEY

As part of your plan, ask teachers to respond to written questions that require them to spend a few minutes describing their thoughts on the subject, drawing out details about PD that may not have been revealed during the face-to-face interviews. For example:

- What has been your experience with PD?
- What did you find most helpful about it? Least helpful?
- What would you most want from a PD program at this school?
- What would you most like to change about how PD is conducted?
- What aspects of your teaching would you like PD to address?
- What aspects of your teaching practice would you like to share in PD meetings?
- What would you like to learn from other teachers during PD meetings?

Your goal with this survey is to find out your staff's comfort levels and what they've experienced in the past—how much PD they've had and their attitudes toward it. Since PD will be the centerpiece of your work as administrator, you must know how your staff reacts to it. You can create a hard-copy survey, or use an online tool like Survey Monkey to create a survey that you administer via email. (On page 57 is a reproducible survey that uses the previous questions.)

ENGAGE STAFF IN TEAMBUILDING EXERCISES

At the start of the school year, teachers have a couple of days when they're not in front of students. That's the time to launch teambuilding activities with your staff. Examples of teambuilding exercises include:

- participating in a wilderness or other outdoor experience to foster teambuilding and cooperation
- participating in activities that demonstrate that people often have more in common than they assume
- participating in activities that demonstrate the satisfaction of being included in a group and the uneasiness of being excluded
- participating in activities that demonstrate the value of team decision-making

Teambuilding exercises push people to interact and work together, creating a spirit of camaraderie, teamwork, collaboration, and a shared vision. Once your staff has that spirit, they'll be more motivated to work together toward your goals, from developing procedures around management and discipline to creating organized structures for each classroom and the school as a whole.

Conducting these exercises also allows you to observe your teachers working together, which will give you valuable information about who's performing well as a team member, and who you'll need to focus on for follow-up conversations one-on-one. Developing a cohesive schoolwide team is not going to happen the first day or in the first couple of days, but you will set the groundwork in those first days.

The crux of this approach is an investment in your school's human capital. The rewards won't be apparent overnight, but they will appear if you keep at it. These small but crucial steps will help you create trusting relationships, establishing the open communication that is essential in improving school performance.

DEVELOP A PLAN OF ACTION

Based on your interviews and surveys, a review of schoolwide data, and a review of attendance trends for students and staff, develop a strategic plan with more specific timelines for the first ninety days of school, including a plan for professional development.

Establish Teams and Keep Communication Lines Open

After you've gathered information and observed staff, you'll be able to see who your teacher leaders are and think about how you can best reach out to them. Meet with these leaders to form teams, such as Instructional Leadership Teams, Grade-Level Teams, and Content Committees. You want to signal to the top performers that you recognize their capabilities. It sends a message that you value their opinions and need them to make the school work better. It's important that people feel this way. When staff feels appreciated, they are more likely to give you their best efforts.

The teams you assemble will vary from school to school. However, I believe that every school should have an Instructional Leadership Team (ILT), a body of people who will look at the data and help you make some wise decisions. The ILT is usually composed of administrators and grade-level chairpersons. They will be your eyes and ears in classrooms, and they will also help communicate and support your goals and vision. (The specifics of forming an ILT are addressed in Chapter Six.)

If you work in a large school, you may also want to set up Grade-Level Teams. For example, if you have three classes for each grade level, it will be much easier for you to call one member of the grade level to a meeting rather than all three teachers. Forming these teams is also an efficient way of getting out information about what's happening in the school to the various grade levels. Your grade-level chairpersons should also be on the ILT.

Content Committees are another type of team you may find useful. They are composed of teachers in the same discipline. For example, having all science teachers on a Content Committee will help you prepare for the school science fair. It's not necessary to have a great number of teams, but you do need ways to manage your staff and get out information in an effective way.

Make an investment in your school's human capital. The rewards won't be apparent overnight, but they will appear if you keep at it.

As you build these teams, continue to keep an open mind about putting the right people in the right places. Someone with expertise in classroom management should be on the schoolwide Behavior Team. Someone who is great with science experiments and has connections to natural history museums should be a part of the Science Team. In some cases, you may have someone who isn't the greatest teacher but who has a very collaborative relationship with other teachers. You've got to work with this person, even if she might not be your first choice for your team. You can coach her to support your vision and be a voice for you among the rest of the staff. In the end, this will strengthen the alliances and alignments on your team.

Once you've selected who's going to be on your core teams, you can begin to teach these teachers and leaders your style of leadership and the way you do things. Share your goals with the core teams, review the data you collected from the information gathering process, and "overly communicate" with team members. By this I mean saying things more than once and in different forms, from meetings to emails to memos.

In addition, don't be tempted to downplay challenges or roadblocks. For example, if data from your one-on-one meetings shows inconsistencies in the enforcement of your schoolwide discipline policy, not enough classroom visits from administration, and a lack of peer observations and collegial visits, share this information with your core teams, and keep the lines of communication open about how you plan to address these issues.

Core Qualities of Effective Teachers

As you evaluate and mentor existing staff and prepare to interview and hire new staff members if necessary, keep in mind the fundamental qualities you'll want to look for and pay special attention to. In this section, I'll explore these core qualities of strong and effective teachers.

COMPETENCE

Alongside classroom management, one of the most important things to consider when you're evaluating a teacher is whether she knows her content area. Some teachers get lost in the classroom if they don't have a book in front of them. You need teachers who are creative and innovative, who know fourth-grade science so well that they can plan lessons without a book, who are resourceful enough to conduct their own research, who can find out if a museum has materials they can use, and who can plan a class trip there. In addition to being creative, resourceful, and innovative, being competent means the teacher is a good manager. She is able to manage the classroom with expectations, routines, and procedures, while creating a positive learning environment where all students are respected and instructional time is maximized.

If you're in a position to bring in new teachers, I caution against hiring someone who doesn't fully know his content area, because he'll always be trying to play catch-up. Unless the teacher is willing to go back to school, it's difficult to scaffold coaching for him in a way that will make a meaningful improvement. Teachers simply have to come into the classroom with that piece in place. As an administrator you can help with management, resources, and creativity, but there is little you can offer a teacher who doesn't know the content.

CHARACTER

It's crucial that you have a feel for a teacher's character in the classroom, and whether she's going to be a positive influence on students. Some teachers have a real gift for treating students with respect and warmth while still maintaining authority in the classroom. A teacher with a positive and vibrant character is good at drawing students out and helping them feel valued as individuals.

On the other side of the coin, the most common character-related issues are teachers treating students negatively and disrespectfully and failing to have cordial, collaborative relations with colleagues and parents. Some teachers go into their classrooms, close their doors, and don't associate with other teachers. They may form cliques and work against the principal or become nasty with other staff members. These attitudes spill into instruction and classroom management, and then parents come to school wanting to know why Ms. Jones doesn't like their children.

With an existing staff, the best way to determine character is by being a regular presence in the classroom. Also, listen to your students and parents. If students are complaining about Mr. Carson saying things he shouldn't be saying, or if parents are complaining about Mr. Carson's classroom behavior, nine times out of ten the students and parents are right. You will need to address those concerns in a critical, difficult conversation with Mr. Carson.

Even when hiring new staff, character can be hard to ascertain. Some people are good at putting on very positive personalities at first, and problems may emerge later. I firmly believe that if your gut tells you no, you should listen. If you have a sense that a person isn't a good fit, most times you'll be right. If you do hire a teacher and then discover challenging character traits, you'll have to take the necessary steps to work with her, at least until you are able to replace her.

CHEMISTRY

Chemistry is the ability work effectively with others. Teachers need to participate in cluster meetings. They need to be able to adapt to parents and work with outside community agents. Improving school performance requires a group of people working as one. A lot of stars make up the galaxy, not just a single star. A teacher who doesn't see himself as a member of the team is not a teacher you want in your school.

Chemistry also hinges on collaboration. Successful collaboration calls for teachers with diverse expertise to work together and engage in shared decision-making toward school goals. It requires that teachers have the ability to jell with other people, and that they don't feel they have all the answers. A teacher may be the number one factor in the classroom, but she can't do it all by herself. She's got to be able to work with other people. Even a teacher who knows the content area backward and forward is not a good fit for your staff unless she's willing to share what she knows in a collaborative way. Over time, an inability to work well with others will create a toxic atmosphere and undermine the school's improvement efforts.

ENERGY

Being a teacher demands great reserves of energy. When you're evaluating a teacher, ask yourself: Does this person have the level of energy and spirit necessary to transform a classroom? Is he really engaged with and committed to improving the student learning process? Or is he always talking about being burned out?

Some of my teachers arrive as early as 6 a.m. and stay until after 6 p.m. Sometimes I have to make them go home. Or when I leave, they're still working. They're involved in extracurricular activities, coaching sports teams, and advising science and art clubs. That's the level of commitment needed, and it requires a high level of energy. But you don't want to see teachers so consistently stressed or overloaded that they burn out. It's important that you support healthy habits to keep teachers balanced and energized rather than drained. Consider creating an Active School Program where staff can participate in fitness classes. Or schedule staff outings for bowling, karaoke, or similar activities to unwind and build camaraderie. Within the school day, give teachers extra preparatory periods whenever possible.

There's no getting around it: To make change happen, teachers must have energy!

FOCUS

Being an effective teacher requires the ability to focus and prioritize in the midst of a busy school and often hectic schedule. When evaluating a staff member, ask yourself: Is this teacher capable of setting priorities and sticking to them? Is she focused on classroom goals? Without clear focus, classroom achievement cannot be raised.

To help create this focus, at the start of the school year ask all of your teachers to set three to five goals for the year. Guide them to select their own priorities for the classroom and hold themselves accountable for areas in which they want to grow. Typical goals could be developing more detailed lesson plans, increasing the pace of lessons, improving the ability to engage students, decreasing teacher talk, or moving from whole-group to small-group instruction. During the school year, periodically revisit these goals, and consider whether they need to be adjusted or if progress is being made toward achieving them. You may want to shape some of your professional development around teacher goals.

COMMITMENT

Another key quality is the intention and ability to follow through on commitments. Your students count on their teachers, and so do you. You can't be everywhere in the school at the same time, so you need to know that your teachers are fully committed to their jobs. It cannot be half-hearted. When teachers don't fulfill their commitments, students begin to lose trust. For many students, school is their place of stability, an environment where there's always going to be safety and consistency, without troubling surprises or changes. The students must be able to trust that the staff will be there for them.

One crucial commitment involves lesson plans. Require your teachers to turn in their plans every week, and make this nonnegotiable. If you don't get lesson plans when they are due, send the teacher a reminder. If that doesn't work, give the teacher a cautionary warning or a written reprimand. Lesson plans have to be a priority. If an emergency arises in a teacher's personal life, you can give him a little leeway. But if turning in lesson plans late becomes a habit, that's a major red flag.

Consider reinforcing this quality further by requiring each teacher to make a commitment to at least one extracurricular activity or program outside of school. And once they have made that commitment, they should stick to it. Again, life is unpredictable and emergencies do happen, but those instances should be rare.

Your responsibility as an instructional leader is not only to receive lesson plans, but also to give teachers comments and notes on them. The teacher's responsibility is to then treat that plan as a living document, and tweak it and work with it based on your feedback. A lot of teachers aren't ready for that responsibility. They may feel that once they've submitted their lesson plans each week, that's it. But in reality, that's just the beginning. Effectively implementing the lesson plan is what lifts student achievement, and teachers have to be committed to going the extra mile to make that happen.

Managing all these responsibilities as an instructional leader requires that you work in teams and delegate responsibility. For example, perhaps you will review lesson plans and monitor classrooms for third through fifth grade, while your assistant principal and Instructional Leadership Team will be responsible for the other grades. You can shift responsibilities throughout the school year, so that eventually you see all lesson plans and classrooms.

JUDGMENT

Sound judgment in dealing with difficult students and parents is essential in improving school performance. Challenging and even confrontational situations have the potential to arise every day during the school year.

Beginning teachers don't always have their judgment down to a science, but they can develop this quality over time. In my experience, the key is to focus on fighting the right battles. It's not effective for a teacher to put students out in the hallway for chewing gum or blow up over something similarly minor. Likewise, a teacher must be able to handle parents when they're upset about a grade, an assignment, or some other issue. If a parent is talking loudly and using profanity, the teacher must be able to deal with it in a respectful way.

 FROM THE PRINCIPAL'S DESK

No matter how well your teachers exercise their judgment, sometimes parents just need to vent in your office. They might have complaints about teachers, but often they'll want advice about parenting. They may be having a rough time at home with their child or simply feeling overwhelmed.

"What would you like for me to do?" I'll ask parents. Most of the time they don't have a specific response. They just need to share their feelings and concerns. If they ask me to fire a teacher, I generally tell them that's not going to happen—at least, not in the near future. I ask them: "What else can we do, right now, so you'll feel better about this?"

Believe it or not, I often view venting by parents in a positive way. It means they see your school as a source of help and a safe place where they can express their views. However, at times, you will need to delegate the responsibility of managing parent feedback or else you will spend too much time putting out these fires.

What parents need to say may not always come out the right way, but they want to be heard and it's important that we listen. Good judgment enables a teacher (or an administrator) to encounter a difficult situation without under- or overreacting. It enables them to give a kind word, calm fears, and maintain respect and authority in such a situation.

Prioritizing Staff Changes

Rarely will you have the luxury of hiring an entirely new staff. Additionally, in most school districts it's very difficult to remove an incompetent teacher once they become tenured. In most cases, you'll need supporting evidence and data to prove why a teacher should be removed, and you may need to provide observation, coaching, and mentorship. If a teacher still fails to improve, only then can she be removed. This process can often take a full year, if not longer.

For all these reasons, it's crucial to devise effective ways to train and improve your existing staff. What kind of plan will help you nurture your teachers? How will you help underperforming teachers rise to the challenge? Once the school year begins, so does the process of monitoring and evaluating your teaching staff. It's important right away to look for signs of problems and do everything you can to address them quickly.

As you evaluate your teachers during the first few weeks of school, you'll find that they fall into six general categories:

1. **Keep in place.** These teachers are working well and are right where you want them to be.
2. **Keep and develop.** You want to keep these teachers where they are, but you need to develop them further through coaching, mentorship, and/or professional development.
3. **Move to another position.** These teachers are not working in the right place and need to be moved to another position or moved to a different classroom with a different set of students.
4. **Observe further.** You're not quite sure about these teachers yet, so you need to observe them for a while longer to determine whether you're going to keep them, develop them, move them to another position, or consider replacing them.

5. **Replace (low priority).** These teachers need to be replaced, but for the time being they're doing no harm. They're not the world's greatest teachers and you don't know how much more you can develop them, but you can deal with them for the school year. During the year, you're going to continually coach this group and have conversations with these teachers. At the end of the year you'll be in a position to say, "Based on the data I collected and documented throughout the year, you just didn't work out for us. Perhaps you want to find a position at a school where you would be a better fit."

6. **Replace (high priority).** If you walk into a classroom and students are hanging from the ceiling and someone is smoking in the back of the room, you need to remove this teacher as quickly as possible. Removal is a complicated process that can take a while, so when you see red flags, start with decisive intervention as close to the beginning of the school year as possible.

You can do many things to improve teacher performance. For example, you can intensively coach a teacher and provide quality professional development. You can have a novice teacher observe an experienced teacher, either in your school or in another school. You can suggest baby steps the teacher can take toward improvement. (You can read about this topic in more detail in Chapters Five and Six.) But if a teacher still doesn't improve, you'll need to have one of your most difficult conversations. Say to the teacher: "I've observed that you've been struggling with management issues all year. While I've tried to support you, I haven't seen the growth I'd like to see. You're not meeting the expectations here." In my experience, after these conversations, many teachers decide to go somewhere else. This is a difficult but necessary step of "minding your building."

Selecting New Staff

Staff turnover differs from school to school. Some teachers retire. Some won't be able to adjust to the changes you want to make and will decide to go elsewhere. Others will be removed after you've evaluated them and determined that they aren't a good fit in your school. Whatever the exact situation, as an administrator, you are responsible for hiring new teachers, so as you evaluate candidates it will be important to remember the core qualities discussed earlier in the chapter. The new teacher you want is talented, resilient, and passionate. He is collaborative. He likes and values young people and has a pleasant character. And he knows his content area inside out.

These teaching qualities would be desirable in any school, but they are particularly necessary in a school that is undertaking major changes in one or more areas. It is essential to have teachers who are collaborative and can form positive relationships with students who are not performing to state standards, who are behind in grade level, or who have special needs. You need teachers who can work well with parents—even with the challenging ones.

HIRING PROCESS FOR NEW STAFF

To hire the right new teachers, carefully design a selection process. The following seven steps will help you with the hiring process.

1. Put together a hiring committee. Send out invitations to staff who might be interested in the committee. If you like, you could also invite parents from your parent-teacher organization or similar group to participate in the process. While your participation in hiring will remain crucial, this team is instrumental in streamlining the process and making sure your time is spent efficiently.

2. Review résumés closely, looking for essential qualifications and experience.

3. Schedule an initial interview with each candidate. Invite other classroom teachers and stakeholders to participate.

4. Invite several candidates for a group interview. Give them a professional reading, and ask the candidates to share their thoughts on the reading and create an action plan in response. Through that group interaction, the personalities of the candidates will begin to show. You'll observe body language, facial expressions, and how the candidates interact with one another, and get snapshots of how your candidates would fit in with your existing team.

5. Schedule a shadowing where candidates follow a teacher around to observe the classroom environment, the school's culture and climate, and instructional rigor.

6. Have each candidate submit a lesson plan. With your team, review the lesson plan. Then give feedback on the plan to the candidate.

Ideally, you'll deliver this feedback in person so you have a chance to observe how the candidate reacts.

7. Schedule a demonstration lesson in which the candidate teaches his submitted lesson plan to a classroom of students. Observe the lesson with your hiring team and provide instructional feedback to the candidate.

This process will help you find the right people for your school—a crucial task. Research confirms that teacher quality is the single most important variable contributing to student achievement.[4] Whether it's a large class or a small class, a lower-performing group of students or a higher-performing group, it is the teacher who will lead students to academic excellence. It is therefore essential that you attract, hire, and develop teachers with the skills to meet the needs of your students.

---

[4] Policy Studies Associates (PSA). "Teacher Quality and Student Achievement: Research Review." Center for Public Education, 2005 (www.centerforpubliceducation.org).

Room for Reflection

EVALUATING YOUR SCHOOL AND STAFF

- What stood out for you in this chapter? Why?
- What new ideas do you have for evaluating your existing staff?
- What will be your biggest challenge in developing a quality staff? How do you propose to address it?
- In what ways are you training and improving existing staff members?

GUIDING QUESTIONS FOR STAFF INTERVIEWS

Colleagues,

Below is a list of questions for our one-on-one conversation. The purpose of these questions is to assist us as we discuss how to continue the powerful teaching and learning that take place at our school, and how we can do even better. Please plan to answer these questions during our scheduled meeting. I look forward to it. Thank you!

What do you believe are the three main strengths of our school?

1. _____
2. _____
3. _____

What aspects of the school do you think are most important to preserve? To change?

_____
_____
_____
_____
_____
_____
_____

What are three key issues we need to work on, in order of importance?

1. _____
2. _____
3. _____

What are the most satisfying aspects of teaching and/or of supporting learning at our school?

_____
_____
_____
_____
_____
_____
_____

What do you need and want from me as your principal?

_____
_____
_____
_____
_____
_____

If you were a new principal coming into this school, what two issues would you tackle first? Discipline? Attendance? Other?

1. _____
2. _____

Among the staff, who do you go to when you need assistance or something done? Why?

_____
_____
_____
_____
_____
_____

Which of your colleagues most inspires you? Who can you count on when you need to get something done? Which teachers do you see as school leaders?

_____
_____
_____
_____
_____
_____

How, in my role as principal, can I be most helpful to you? What do you need me to do to support you?

_____
_____
_____
_____
_____
_____

STAFF PROFESSIONAL DEVELOPMENT SURVEY

The goal of this survey is to find out your comfort levels and past experiences with professional development (PD). Since PD will be the centerpiece of our work together, your answers will help us design the PD plan that will be most useful to you and to our school.

What has been your past experience with PD?

_____

_____

_____

What did you find most helpful about it? Least helpful?

_____

_____

_____

What would you most want from a PD program at this school?

_____

_____

_____

What would you most like to change about how PD is conducted?

_____

_____

_____

What aspects of your teaching would you like PD to address?

_____

_____

_____

What aspects of your teaching practice would you like to share in PD meetings?

_____

_____

_____

What would you like to learn from other teachers during PD meetings?

_____

_____

_____

CHAPTER FOUR

Culture and Climate—Establishing a Positive, Safe, and Nurturing Environment

Every school has its own look, sound, and feel—a unique atmosphere and mood. Yet without a sense of order, safety, and security, students cannot learn effectively. When a school has a positive, safe, and nurturing environment, it sends the message that the school is student-focused and students are coming there to learn. Not surprisingly, research shows that students perform better in such an environment.[5] Especially in struggling or under-performing schools, administrators often confront an environment of low expectations for student performance, major disciplinary issues, teacher cynicism, student distrust, rowdy classrooms, and unstructured hallways and lunchrooms. Whatever the starting point, however, transforming culture can be a challenge—one that you'll need to face and overcome if you are going to succeed in your mission. So the question then becomes: how do we teach young people to "do school," and how can we create the culture and climate we want to see?

A school's culture is created and affected by a wide variety of factors, ranging from such large issues as how discipline is handled, how classrooms are managed, and how teachers view their jobs, to seemingly smaller issues such as how students enter the building in the morning, how they walk the hallways during and between classes, how teachers address students, and the appearance of classrooms, hallways, and lunchrooms. When I first became a principal, my initial conversations with teachers made it clear to me that we needed to change the school's atmosphere before we could successfully teach dynamic lessons in any subject. Since then, I've come to firmly believe that it's a mistake to introduce new academic content or methods until students understand the school's behavioral expectations, and until they learn to walk the hallways quietly, respect each other, and sit in their seats. Such

---

[5] *International Journal of Leadership in Education*, Jan–March 2009, Vol. 12, No. 1, 73–84.

expectations are key to transforming any school. In this chapter, I'll walk you through some of the principles and practices you can draw on as you work toward your culture and climate goals.

FROM THE PRINCIPAL'S DESK

In the summer before I became a principal, I engaged staff in five weeks of professional development training, during which we fleshed out our plan for changing the school's culture and climate. Starting in September and continuing well into November, we concentrated on implementing that plan. Satisfied with the changes we had made, we were ready to turn up the intensity of instruction. When students came back from the Thanksgiving and winter breaks, we gave them a refresher course on our rules and expectations. Each time they returned from a holiday or break, it got easier to maintain the culture we'd established, because we had spent quality time at the start of the year making sure that everyone—both students and staff—understood our rules and expectations. Later, a charter school principal from Washington, D.C., asked me to describe my main focus during my first year as a principal. I told her without hesitation that my first priority had been creating a positive, safe, and nurturing culture and climate for the students. Without that environment, I knew we couldn't improve academic performance.

Developing Expectations, Routines, and Systems

Changing a school's culture involves changing attitudes, routines, and systems, and this can be a tall order. But there is a clear method you can follow. How and where do you begin, as an administrator, to address this crucial issue?

In my experience, Positive Behavioral Interventions and Supports (PBIS) is a powerful system for organizing a school community. PBIS is not a mandated program, but it is used by many schools. It is not a packaged program or a binder with a "how-to" curriculum, but a set of general guidelines for the process you should go through with your staff, asking and answering questions such as:

- What will be the core values and behavioral expectations for all students?
- What practices will we need to put in place to achieve and maintain those expectations?
- How will we identify and define problems and skill deficits in behavior?

- What structures and systems will we need to implement to acknowledge or recognize the expected behavior?
- How will we teach, model, practice, and acknowledge the behaviors we expect?
- Where, when, and why are certain behaviors occurring?
- What will be the procedures and systems for handling inappropriate behavior?
- How will we monitor implementation? What data will we use, how will we gather it, and how will we use it?

PBIS provides overarching guidance for improving student behavior. However, as an administrator, you'll still need to develop the specific programs and strategies to put that guidance into action. If you're using PBIS at your school, you'll address student behavior by grouping students into three tiers: universal, secondary, and tertiary. What tier a student falls into is based on the severity of that student's behavior issues and need for support. If a student generally complies with the rules of the school and for the most part has appropriate school behavior, he or she would fall into the universal category, or Tier 1, which in my experience generally amounts to 80 percent of the student body. While these students do not have major behavior issues, they can still benefit from universal-level interventions such as Second Step, a PBIS-recommended training that teaches appropriate social behavior and how to build relationships with fellow students.

When the data shows that a child has greater numbers of infractions and inappropriate behaviors, that child will likely move into Tier 2, where she will receive more services and support. Interventions at the secondary level might include Check-In/Check-Out, a targeted PBIS intervention for Tier 2. Other supports at this level could include interventions to help students cope with anger, along with conflict resolution processes such as Restorative Conversations and Talking Circles.

When you have a student whose data shows a very high number of inappropriate behaviors, and especially when those behaviors are interfering with academics, that child moves into the Tier 3 category. Such students will need more support, probably in the form of counseling or an Individualized Education Program (IEP). The IEP may indicate that students have certain emotional or behavioral triggers and suggest ways to deal with these challenges.

One of the most important points made by PBIS is that teachers and staff must model the appropriate behavior they want to see. They can't assume students know how to behave or that they will learn to do so from a simple, one-time explanation. Just as academic deficiencies have to be identified and corrected systematically, some behavior deficiencies need to be addressed through careful instruction and modeling.

Whether your school implements PBIS or not, you can still use its general ideas as starting points and guidance. For instance, here are four main steps you can take to develop a healthy culture and climate:

- Develop core values
- Define a matrix of behaviors
- Model and implement the behaviors
- Teach the expected behaviors

As an administrator, it's important to have a strong vision of the culture and climate you're working toward. Don't go into a team meeting about this issue with a blank slate. Instead, walk in with clear ideas of what you want to see in your school, but then allow your team to question these ideas, provide feedback on goals, and give shape to your schoolwide vision.

Core Principles and Practices for Creating a Positive School Culture

As you and your team strive to create and sustain a positive, safe, and nurturing school culture, you can draw upon and develop the core principles and practices explored in the rest of this chapter.

IDENTIFY AND DEVELOP CORE SCHOOL VALUES

Your school's core values will be a source of guidance, inspiration, and motivation all year round. If possible, start the process of identifying these values during the summer. Engage your staff in fleshing out your plan for culture and climate, and use this plan as a starting point for developing specific schoolwide values for students, using the guidance of PBIS if you like.

PBIS advises that schools establish three or four core values, instead of having dozens of rules that are punitive in nature. For example:

Great School Academy Core Values

Respect Yourself

Respect Others

Respect Your Environment

Respect Teaching and Learning

Next, develop a general statement of principle for staff, such as:

It is the goal of Great School Academy to promote positive and appropriate behaviors and consistent and appropriate discipline. The staff will use discipline data to identify patterns and possible causes of inappropriate behavior. This information will then be used to develop effective interventions to decrease inappropriate behavior and increase desired behavior within the school.

Using your core values and your statement of principle as guides, develop specific staff goals for culture and climate. These goals might include expectations such as the following:

- Staff must be able to identify the whereabouts of every student for safety purposes.
- Staff will view inappropriate behavior in the same manner as problems in reading or math—as a skill deficit. When a skill deficit exists, we must model and teach the appropriate skill. When a behavior deficit exists, we do the same.
- Staff will identify behavior patterns to design strategies/interventions for improvement.
- Staff will promote a sense of responsibility on the part of students, parents, and staff to insure maximum compliance by all students.
- Great School Academy will decrease student misconducts by one half.

Be aware that if your school has high numbers of discipline referrals and issues, those numbers could actually increase in the first few months as you implement tighter standards. This happened in two schools where I was the new administrator. Those higher numbers are a sign that the old discipline standards were too lax. Try not to become frustrated or discouraged by this spike. Instead, focus on the long-term changes and cultural shift you're striving toward.

MAKE EXPECTATIONS TRANSPARENT TO EVERYONE

The next step is to make your expectations about culture and climate clear and transparent to both students and parents. One straightforward approach to begin this process is to conduct a behavior assembly at the start of the school year. At this assembly, administrators and teachers can model behavior for the students, as well as review the student handbook (having made sure that every student received one during the first week).

Some schools create specific student handbooks for each grade or group of grades (such as preK to second grade; third to fifth grade; and sixth to eighth grade). In other schools, students might have agenda books in which the first five to ten pages list school expectations, including a sign-off sheet for parents to affirm that they've read and understood the rules. Whatever system your school uses, the key goal is to ensure that your expectations of students are clear and that they have been understood by students as well as by their caregivers and guardians.

You might be thinking that this kind of consistent and systematic approach to discipline is not the norm in many schools. In a surprising number of classrooms, everyone is winging it most of the time, and a common response to infractions is, "I'm going to call your parents." Winging it and inconsistency won't change the culture of a school from the inside out.

Another way to make your expectations clear is by addressing students directly and informing them about the details of your guidelines, goals, and requirements. For instance, at the start of the school year, I speak at an assembly and tell students about behavioral expectations in various areas of our building. We also post that information for them in the hallways, so there's no wiggle room for students to say they didn't know the rules. Just as my teachers have anchor charts in their classrooms—visual presentations of lessons that students can refer back to for help—we also have charts about expectations in the hallways and bathrooms. Students are completely clear about how to behave on the way to an assembly or to the restroom. If they happen to forget, the reminder is on the wall:

- A Great School Academy student is in a straight line.
- A Great School Academy student keeps his hands to himself.
- A Great School Academy student has a voice level of zero.

I know that these rules may sound rigid to some administrators, and I'm not suggesting a one-size-fits-all approach. The schools where I have served as an administrator required this approach to discipline. And at the time, some parents did feel that some of our routines were too rigid and "like the military." However, those initial concerns dissolved after families visited the school a few times and not only saw the benefits of discipline, but also realized that grades and test scores were on the rise.

Still, not every school requires this approach. You must determine your own approaches, based on your own students, staff, and community.

FROM THE PRINCIPAL'S DESK

In my school, while our rules are very clear, there aren't a lot of **don'ts**. Everything is phrased in a positive way. In addition to expectations, we have artwork in the hallways, high school banners, college banners, and inspirational quotes. We make it clear that our goal is student success.

CREATE A CARING COMMUNITY

As discussed in the previous chapter, one of your first priorities is hiring staff that offer students and parents acceptance, respect, warmth, and partnership.

However, even if you don't have the luxury of hiring a new staff and screening them for the exact traits you want, you can still create a caring community with your existing staff. Talk with staff about accepting students the way they are. Everyone who enters a classroom should be respected. Students should be addressed in a caring tone, and parents should feel a sense of warmth and partnership from the teachers as well as from the administration. And as a visible, hands-on leader, you can model these behaviors for your teachers and staff.

You may have worked in overcrowded schools—or you may work in such a school now. Sometimes, when teachers feel overwhelmed by their class sizes, they can struggle to put forth a warm and positive attitude. I've seen parents arrive with newly enrolled students—with both the parents and students feeling a mix of excitement and apprehension—only to have teachers make it obvious that they aren't pleased about the addition. It may seem like a small moment, but consider what kind of message it sends. The parent's first impression is that his child isn't welcome because the teacher looks unhappy.

You can help your staff—whether they're new hires or long-time team members—become aware of how these seemingly minor interactions can affect your school's culture in a significant way. Talk with teachers and other staff about how they react to certain situations when they're especially busy or stressed. You could even role-play possible scenarios in special staff meetings to help people consider how they might send messages without even realizing it, and how they could respond more positively. In too many schools, teachers don't give students the sense that they will do their best to help them succeed.

In a positive school culture, all adults model caring behavior that says to parents, "I like young people. I am a caring person, and I will nurture and support your child. I'm going to make sure that your child is safe, and I'm going to notify you about both good and bad behavior."

Teachers must show through words and actions that they genuinely care about students and value them as individuals.

Of course, sometimes these can be empty promises. Teachers also must show through words and actions that they genuinely care about students and value them as individuals. And teachers will take their cues from *you* about how to conduct themselves. If they habitually fail to show respect and caring, it's time to initiate a difficult conversation.

ESTABLISH APPROPRIATE RULES AND CONSEQUENCES FOR BEHAVIOR

Establishing clear and consistent rules and consequences for inappropriate behavior is crucial in improving and maintaining a positive school culture. PBIS also recommends forming a Behavior Health Team (BHT), also known as a discipline committee. At BHT meetings, a child's academic record, his family dynamic, and anecdotal information about his behavior are all brought to the table as the team discusses next steps in a disciplinary referral. Not every school will have a BHT, but you do need some kind of behavior-focused team to look at the discipline data and develop plans for decreasing inappropriate behavior. You might have a BHT that includes all of your clinicians, or a discipline committee comprised of teachers and education support personnel (ESPs or teacher assistants).

However you structure this behavior-focused group, part of the team's work should be to identify a list of specific behaviors that will result in disciplinary action. Developing this list works well as a collaborative, brainstorming team effort. Teachers can rattle off incidents that disrupt instructional time and can give important feedback about how the administration should handle certain infractions. Meanwhile, the BHT or discipline committee should be checking in with you to keep you informed, and to brainstorm ideas or troubleshoot situations when your input is necessary. I recommend attending all of your BHT meetings, if possible. However, you will need to decide—based on your school and its needs—what to prioritize and which teams you want to be most actively involved with.

Whether or not you're using PBIS, I recommend creating a schoolwide behavior matrix. Each grade level should have the same schoolwide behavior matrix, so every teacher in the school is working together and enforcing the same, consistent policy. But each teacher will also create her own classroom behavior management plan (sometimes called a Behavior Management Cycle or BMC) in support of that consistent, overarching matrix. This unique classroom plan will include whatever details the teacher feels are important for her students beyond those on the schoolwide matrix. And a first-grade BMC is going to look different from one used in fifth or eighth grade because of differences in age, types of problems, and expectations. A sample schoolwide matrix appears in Figure 3 on page 67.

CREATE A CLEAR AND CONSISTENT REFERRAL SYSTEM, AND KEEP GOOD RECORDS

A key element of managing behavior issues is setting up a clear referral system with a schoolwide form that you use consistently in addressing and recording infractions. If you don't already have such a form, you can use the Discipline Referral Form included as a reproducible on pages 90–91. Whenever a behavior problem occurs—even if it is minor—have the relevant staff member fill out this Discipline Referral Form. Recording discipline concerns, even when an issue has been addressed, makes for good record keeping and data collection.

I advise using this form in triplicate. In too many busy schools, a teacher makes a referral, the student goes to the office, and the teacher is left wondering what happened. You can prevent this breakdown in communication by consistently using your Discipline Referral Form, and by always promptly distributing copies to the administration, the teacher, and the

FIGURE 3: SAMPLE SCHOOLWIDE BEHAVIOR MATRIX

	Hallways	Bathroom	Playground	Doorway Procedures	Assemblies	Café/Lunchroom	Resource/Specialty Lab
Respect Yourself	• Stay quiet while in single-file line. • If you are spoken to, respond using appropriate language. • Walk slowly—no running. • Keep your hands to yourself.	• Keep the bathroom clean. • Always wash your hands before leaving the bathroom.	• Demonstrate good sportsmanship. • Use appropriate, respectful language. • Use equipment appropriately and keep it clean.	• Be silent upon entrance. • Line up single-file.	• Listen and watch quietly. • Be a good participant. • Be courteous to others.	• Line up single-file for enter and exit. • Stay seated until dismissed. • Practice good manners. • Keep at least eight inches between yourself and others.	• Show respect to all adults at all times. • Ask for help when you need it.
Respect Others	• Use an appropriate tone of voice. • Respect others' space. • Listen and follow adult directions at all times. • Notice and appreciate bulletin board displays and wall ornaments.	• Respect others' privacy. • Keep your hands and feet to yourself. • Observe time limits.	• Be patient and wait your turn. • Play safely. • Play by the rules of the games.	• Give others their space. • Line up single-file.	• Applaud appropriately. • Keep your hands and feet to yourself.	• Smile and wave at others. • Place garbage in trash cans. • Eat your own food. • Sit at your assigned table.	• Respect others' space.
Respect Your Environment	• Use trash receptacles. • Help keep walls clean. • Value and respect bulletin boards or wall ornaments.	• Use trash receptacles. • Remember to flush. • Treat school property with care. • Help keep walls clean.	• Use trash receptacles. • Dispose of gum properly. • Keep school property clean.	• Allow traffic to flow past you when you stop. • Be courteous. • Only bring appropriate materials and supplies to school.	• Help keep seats and walls in good condition. • Dispose of gum properly.	• Help keep seats and tables in good condition. • Keep your area clean.	• Help keep equipment clean. • Use equipment appropriately.
Respect Teaching & Learning	• Eat and drink in the lunchroom only. • Arrive at your class on time (prompt and prepared). • Have agenda book as a pass.	• Follow appropriate bathroom procedures. • Observe time limits. • Be sure to have your agenda book as a pass.	• Stay in the playground area. • Stop your activity when you hear the whistle. • Listen and respond politely. • Line up quietly.	• Respond to adult directions. • Arrive on time. • Use appropriate language during entrance and exit.	• Sit in your assigned area. • Listen and be cooperative. • Follow entry and dismissal routes. • Follow adult directions.	• Use a quiet voice at all times. Keep your area clean. • Listen to lunch supervisors. Say "please" and "thank you" to the people who help you.	• Bring the necessary books and other materials or supplies.

parents or caregivers. Then everyone is up to date and on the same page. Everyone knows that an incident happened on November 3, and that a specific action was taken on November 4.

A clear referral system also provides you with useful data. You don't want teachers referring students for disciplinary action with no transparent explanation of what action was taken. And you don't want to try to determine appropriate consequences for a student without some knowledge of her history.

When you're establishing disciplinary procedures, make sure that you and your team give every child the opportunity to redeem herself. She may have misbehaved today, but tomorrow is a new day. All students should be given chances to start over and not be punished for what they did yesterday. In this way, they can be taught self-discipline, so they learn that if they are able to control their impulses, they can have a fresh start.

Of course, some students are repeat offenders, and parents need to know when that is the case. When a serious or repeat offense takes place, teachers must contact parents or caregivers before the situation reaches your office. When teachers don't do that, parents may then complain that you neglected to inform them that their child was having a problem. And in general, most parents appreciate getting notified very early on about any behavior problems.

As you get used to keeping parents and guardians in the loop, another thing you'll need to decide is how available you are willing to be—or should be—to parents during out-of-school hours. Similarly, your teachers will have to make the same decision for themselves. I don't give my personal cell phone number to parents, but some of my teachers do. They're in regular contact with one another, maintaining open and constant communication about the students. And of course, parents do have my school phone number and email address, so that they can communicate with me through those channels.

SPLIT UP RESPONSIBILITY FOR BEHAVIOR MANAGEMENT

Another part of setting up your referral system is determining which behavior issues will be classroom-managed and which will be administration-managed. The form on pages 90–91 gives one way to break this down—listing teacher-managed issues on one side and administration-managed issues on the other—but you may choose to handle certain infractions differently in your school. Along these same lines, once something happens in class that takes away from instructional time and a teacher responds but that response is not effective, then what? How is the school going to handle the situation? Without a clear demarcation of responsibility, either teachers or administration can end up being over-whelmed by disciplinary procedures.

In the following sections, you'll read a description of one approach to splitting up these responsibilities.

TEACHER-MANAGED

Many behavior issues will be best handled by teachers in their individual classrooms. With your staff, you can decide what constitutes teacher-managed behavior. It doesn't hurt to give a few examples to new teachers during your group meetings to help compile these lists. But experienced teachers won't have a problem identifying typical infractions, which usually include:

- Chewing gum or eating candy
- Not having supplies
- Being tardy or absent
- Excessive talking
- Throwing small objects
- Sleeping in class
- Minor stealing
- Working off-task
- Taking part in a minor altercation (such as running, pushing, or horseplay)
- Being disruptive in the classroom or hallway
- Being disrespectful
- Refusing to follow directions
- Cheating or plagiarizing
- Profanity
- A single use of a cell phone or other electronic device

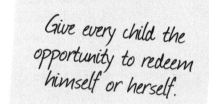

Give every child the opportunity to redeem himself or herself.

As you and your team establish which behaviors will be teacher-managed, you can also develop a set of specific and detailed steps that teachers use in their response, so that everyone in the school knows the order in which behavior should be addressed. For example:

Step 1: The classroom teacher observes the problem behavior.

Step 2: The problem behavior is challenged and corrected using classroom management rules and consequences. The teacher fills out a Discipline Referral Form for his records and distributes it to the administration and to the student's parents or guardians. The teacher also keeps one form for himself.

Step 3: The teacher makes additional direct contact with parents through telephone calls, teacher conferences, and/or notes sent home.

Step 4: The teacher keeps a classroom record of misconduct and consequences.

While it's important for you and your team to discuss ideas for these practices and procedures, you may also want to give each of your teachers the freedom to use her own behavior management plan within her classroom and to establish her own classroom method, within the general structure you've established for handling classroom behavior. Figure 4 on page 71 shows an example of the type of plan that a teacher might create.

Teachers can use a variety of tools and techniques to address discipline, depending on what they're most comfortable with. But whatever their approach, they must teach the school's expected behaviors. Furthermore, they must have a plan for when a child doesn't comply. A teacher can't simply send a child out of the classroom the first time he makes a mistake. Instead, in a primary classroom, the first response might be a timeout. Or it could be a warning for a first infraction, a timeout for a second infraction, and a phone call and a note sent home for a third infraction. Flexibility in this area is fine, as long as each teacher has a plan that you have reviewed. Tactics might include warnings, alternative recess, and calling home. Some teachers display their students' behavior on a color-coded chart in the classroom. Then each student knows exactly where she is and can see when she improves.

If a child exhausts all of the options within a teacher's plan, that's when the child enters the administration-managed behavior plan, which I'll describe in the next section. In the event that a child's behavior is extremely disruptive, the teacher may choose to bypass her usual management system and immediately move a child into the administration-managed behavior plan.

FIGURE 4: SAMPLE TEACHER BEHAVIOR MANAGEMENT PLAN

Morning	Transitions	Dismissal	Procedures
ENTRY • Students line up at the designated third-grade spot on the playground. • Teacher picks up students in two single-file lines. • Students enter carefully and silently. • Students maintain a voice level of 0. • Students have 15 minutes to eat breakfast, put away personal belongings, and prepare materials for the first period. **BREAKFAST** • Students will pick up bags as they enter the building from their designated locations. • Once in the classroom, students have 15 minutes to eat and clean up. **ATTENDANCE** • The teacher takes attendance and puts it into the gradebook while students are having breakfast. **MORNING WORK** • "Do Now" activities are clearly posted and worksheets are ready for distribution before students enter the room. • Students work on these short activities while eating breakfast.	**STOPPING ACTIVITY** • At the start of the activity, students will be verbally told what the end time will be. • The teacher will use a timer to let students know time is up and to start preparing personal belongings for the next activity or period. **GETTING STUDENTS' ATTENTION** • The teacher will use the universal hand signal. • The teacher will follow the hand signal with power claps if needed. **MOVEMENT TO SEATS** • Students move carefully and silently. • Students maintain a voice level of 0.	**STOPPING ACTIVITY** • Students will have 5 minutes to prepare their personal belongings. • Teacher will call each table one at a time to line up and/or get any additional belongings from closet. • During these 5 minutes, students are careful and silent. • Students maintain a voice level of 0. **HOMEWORK AND NOTES** • Homework will be assigned and notes will be passed out during the last 10 minutes of the class period. • Students copy homework in their agendas or notebooks. • Each student has a homework folder for notes and worksheets. **EXITING BUILDING** • Students exit carefully and silently in two lines. • Students maintain a voice level of 0. • Students exit from the same doors they entered in the morning.	**GETTING SUPPLIES** • Classroom jobs are assigned weekly, such as line leaders, table leaders, soap monitors, washroom monitors, and paper passers who will help the teacher prepare, collect, and distribute necessary materials. **LINING UP** • Students move carefully and silently. • Students maintain a voice level of 0. **WALKING THROUGH THE HALLWAYS** • Students move carefully and silently. • Students maintain a voice level of 0. **PUTTING AWAY MATERIALS** • The last 5 minutes are for cleanup and preparing personal belongings for next period or activity. • Students maintain a voice level of 0. • Weekly assigned table leaders will help the teacher prepare, collect, and distribute necessary materials. **EXITING THE CLASSROOM** • Students move carefully and silently. • Students maintain a voice level of 0. • The teacher will give verbal commands to proceed and stop as needed.

FROM THE PRINCIPAL'S DESK

Occasionally, you might run into this situation: A student may not have behaved inappropriately, but a teacher has simply reached her limit. When this happens in my school, administration might take the child out of class for a few minutes, but we try to send that child back as soon as possible. I remind my teachers that instructional time is precious, and we have to maximize it. Whenever a child isn't in the classroom, he is missing out on a chance to learn.

ADMINISTRATION-MANAGED

It's important to have a clear disciplinary system that addresses the many different types of behavior that can occur in a classroom. Teacher-managed issues would be eating in the classroom, continually showing up without supplies, or talking in class or the hallway. Teachers should be able to handle minor problems that "come with the classroom."

For example, a teacher shouldn't send a student out of the classroom for taking a pencil from another student's desk. By contrast, an administration-managed behavior would be using profanity toward a teacher, bringing a weapon to school, or starting a fight. Major or flagrant behavior issues that are extremely disruptive to the classroom should be administration-managed. Just as you've done with the teacher-managed behaviors, you should work with your team to compile a list of administration-managed issues, which might include the following:

- Skipping class or leaving school
- Writing notes that contain lewd or threatening content
- Fighting
- Having a weapon at school
- Possessing or being under the influence of tobacco or drugs
- Multiple uses of a cell phone or other electronic device
- Property damage
- Theft
- Bullying, intimidation, or physical threats
- Sexual harassment
- Defiance or major disrespect of authority
- Gang-related activity

- Excessive profanity or profanity directed at adults
- Threats against staff or students

Here are sample steps you might use for administration-managed referrals.

Step 1: The classroom teacher observes the problem behavior.

Step 2: The problem behavior has been challenged using classroom management rules and consequences but has not been corrected.

Step 3: The teacher writes a Discipline Referral Form and submits it to the appropriate administrative staff, as well as preparing a copy to send to the student's parents or guardians. In emergency cases, a patrolling security officer may take the student and the referral directly to the administration. In other cases of emergency, the teacher can contact the office via the classroom intercom system for immediate assistance.

Step 4: Consequences are determined by the administration.

Step 5: The teacher and/or administrators make additional direct contact with parents or guardians through telephone calls, teacher conferences, and/or notes sent home.

Step 6: The administration files the necessary documentation, records all referrals, and informs the teacher of the outcome.

It is crucial that everyone knows what the administration-managed steps will be. When transparency is lacking, teachers and parents are likely to complain that they don't know what happened after a child was removed from the classroom. When the student returns to the classroom, the teacher might think that no consequences were imposed, and may feel angry at not being supported by the administration.

By contrast, when you do have transparency, a parent will come to the school for a conference with both the administration and the teacher to discuss and explain what happened. In the end, the parent will know the exact consequences for his child, and the teacher won't be left in the dark about how the administration handled the problem.

Once you have established schoolwide values and procedures, talk with your staff at the start of the school year about discipline and classroom management, and what your referral system will be. One approach you could take is to give teachers a list of the specific disciplinary issues that will be managed by the administration. Everything else, they are responsible for. Again, I don't expect teachers to send me students who don't have notebook paper or are chewing gum. Those kinds of issues should be teacher-managed. Laying out clear and detailed guidelines for their responsibilities in improving culture and climate will empower them to manage their own classrooms in the ways most efficient and effective for them.

TAKE YOUR CULTURE INTO ACCOUNT

As you develop your school's behavior expectations—and the consequences for not meeting those expectations—don't be afraid to dig into the details. And as you do so, consider your school culture and the wider community, as well as what your teachers are personally comfortable with.

For example, you may want to define—in detail—what profanity your teachers can consider minor and what they'll view as major. A second grader may say "damn" because his mom says it at home. You wouldn't write up a second grader for saying that, just as you wouldn't write up a second grader for making a mistake on a test. But if profanity is directed toward an adult, the administration should know about it. That student can receive an intervention addressing the problem, making it clear the language was not appropriate, and showing him that he can choose to use other words. Be clear and intentional about what you will allow and what you won't.

Similarly, the use of electronics is another area where you'll have to set specific parameters based on your community and culture. At my school, we collect cell phones at the start of the day and return them before dismissal. We don't want kids chatting on Facebook or Instagram, or talking on their phones. Once again, your decisions will be based on how much you need or want to manage. By collecting phones, you also don't have to deal with the issue of phones being stolen. If a phone isn't turned in, the child is responsible if it's lost. If parents are concerned about a safety issue they can call the school, but they can't call their children on their cell phones. Whatever policy you choose to institute, explain it clearly at the beginning of the school year, and enforce it consistently throughout the remainder of the year.

If you proactively create school and classroom norms at the start of the year, you'll avoid having to deal with many of the minor problems that can

FROM THE PRINCIPAL'S DESK

At the start of the year, I like to send home letters saying, "During the first couple of weeks of school, we are going to be introducing new expectations for building a positive school culture and climate." You may want to adopt a similar practice. It gives you an opportunity to get students and parents on board with the mindset that what may have been accepted in the past will not be accepted anymore. It's also your chance to prepare parents for the reality that you intend to be strict about upholding expectations. You may even want to call parents or invite them to the school, so that everyone in the school community is on the same page. In addition, if you're working with students and families who aren't used to structure and process at school, you can send similar letters at additional times during the year reminding everyone of your common goals. At these times you can also "start over" if you've encountered challenges and rough patches along the way. Along with the beginning of the school year, this can be done after holiday breaks in January or the spring.

arise from day to day, and you'll give your teachers the trust and the agency they need to be responsible for their classrooms.

HAVE TEACHERS DEVELOP CLASSROOM MANAGEMENT PLANS

At the beginning of the year—before the first day of school, if possible—require each of your teachers to develop a plan for managing her classroom behavior. Provide staff with your overarching goals for culture and climate, along the lines I've discussed: that students respect each other and themselves, respect the school environment, and respect teaching and learning. Using these as a starting point, make each teacher responsible for coming up with a specific classroom plan for her students. You need to know how your teachers are going to transfer your goals, in specific and concrete ways, into their classrooms. How will each teacher reinforce routines and procedures based on your school's core values in the classroom? What will those routines and procedures look like?

Next, ask each teacher to create a Teacher Behavior Management Plan describing the steps they will take when a student shows either appropriate or inappropriate behavior. All teachers must answer specific questions in detail:

• How are you going to run your classroom?
• How will the classroom become a community?

- What will you do when a child takes a pencil from another student? Are you going to give the child a warning or a timeout? Sit with the child at lunch? Call home?
- How are you teaching and modeling appropriate behavior?
- What specific tools, strategies, and interventions are you using in pursuit of these goals? (For example, you might use Second Step lessons to help students respond appropriately and manage their emotions, or Cool Tools lesson plans to teach behavioral expectations in various parts of the school.)

Teachers can answer these questions in writing, in face-to-face meetings, or both. Discuss these questions during orientation for teachers at the start of the school year. Also include your disciplinary procedures in the staff handbook, pointing out what you want teachers to do—and what you don't want them to do. Share what you expect to see in their behavior plans, including examples of actions they will take (and not take) in certain situations. You can have follow-up, face-to-face meetings with teachers if you don't understand something in their behavior plans.

Again, some teachers and parents may see these approaches as overly rigid, and the approaches you take will need to be based on your school culture. Some schools and some communities need a highly organized way of addressing discipline. But you can adapt these methods of addressing behavior to fit your school's climate and culture.

PAY ATTENTION TO YOUR DATA

If you use PBIS to collect data on schoolwide behavior, you probably already keep data on specific students and infractions. Another way of recording data is to record where misconducts are happening. If you're getting twenty-five referrals during lunch and recess, that's a trend that needs attention. Do you need more staff in the cafeteria? Should table assignments be switched around? Do you have the right rules in place to maintain order?

Similarly, if Mr. Romero has ten disciplinary referrals in two days, that's a problem. You will need to pay a friendly visit to Mr. Romero to make sure he's working from his behavior management plan, and using appropriate interventions effectively.

When a student is brought to you, the Discipline Referral Form must indicate whether the student is a repeat offender. This helps staff and parents determine if there's a pattern that needs to be addressed. It will also help in IEP conferences, when a child might be considered for special education. Finally, this referral system holds teachers accountable because they can't put students in the hallway or take other disciplinary action without a documented reason.

To keep your behavior issues in check and keep the majority of your students from needing more targeted and intense interventions, make sure you're looking at your data and paying attention to those students who are complying with your rules and core values. Additionally, be sure to initiate schoolwide incentives for positive behaviors. For instance, in return for helping another student, demonstrating appropriate behavior in the lunchroom, or being quiet in the halls, you could offer tokens usable in the school store. However you choose to acknowledge the actions you want to see, it's just as important to reward good behaviors as it is to correct inappropriate ones.

PROMOTE RESTORATIVE JUSTICE PRACTICES AND SIMILAR TOOLS

A nationwide movement in education calls for principals and schools to exhaust every opportunity before taking a child out of school as a disciplinary action. To work toward this goal, it's common for a team consisting of a social worker, a case manager, a counselor, a psychologist, and a clinical psychologist to provide services and restorative practices. This group will consider all the issues affecting the child. Then, based on the data, they will decide if the child needs to participate in an intervention such as a peace circle (restorative conversations), Check In/Check Out (a PBIS Tier 2 intervention), an anger coping intervention, a peer jury, community service, more time one-on-one with a social worker or psychologist, or some other method of addressing the issue.

For instance, if two kids argue, rather than receiving detention or a silent lunch, they might take part in a peace circle. In this out-of-class intervention, a teacher sits down with the students who argued and moderates a conversation about what happened. The students discuss their behavior and feelings, and make peace with each other so that instructional time in the classroom can be maximized. Such conversations are often ongoing.

PBIS and other systems won't necessarily give you the script for peace circles or other conversations within restorative justice. You and your teachers need to decide how to have these discussions. For example, in my school, if a student has done something that merits an apology, my dean will walk the student around to classes. The student may not have to say anything to the entire class, but will definitely have a conversation with the teacher. This approach doesn't take long, but it goes a long way toward building responsibility and accountability.

Anger coping interventions are another practice you can use. These group sessions bring together students who, based on the data, are combative and could be explosive. In one of these interventions, a social worker or counselor leads a conversation with these students about what makes them angry, so both teachers and students can learn their triggers. In addition to this exploration of root causes, counselors will also give the students strategies to cope with their anger. In some cases, they will also offer teachers ideas for addressing a student's anger before it gets out of control.

It's just as important to reward good behaviors as it is to correct inappropriate ones.

Peer juries are also a useful tool, especially in upper-grade classrooms and high school. If a student has committed an infraction, she sits in a room with a group of peers who ask questions about what the student did. The peers then describe how the student's behavior affected the school community. In some schools, the peer jury may decide what the consequences will be, according to specific school guidelines. They can recommend community service, such as helping out at a community center or picking up trash around the neighborhood, or the student making a public apology to the class. This process works to bring more students into the process of holding students accountable for their actions.

These are just a few of the many innovative methods administrators use today to address and correct behavior issues, with expulsion being the absolute last resort. Expulsion in many cases denies the student of his education for a period of time. Once a child leaves public school, he may not be enrolled in alternative classes, and this can create or widen gaps in his learning. He is likely to fall farther and farther behind. Additionally, when expelled students are not receiving the appropriate services or supports to correct their behavior, they may stray into deeper trouble. So, whenever possible, it is critical to avoid expulsion and keep students in school where they receive not only academic instruction but also behavioral, social, and emotional supports to help make them better members of society.

PBIS and other systems give some guidance on appropriate tools, but you'll need to adapt these tools to fit your school's needs. Trust in your teachers' creativity and expertise. While you should be able to offer them ideas and solutions if they cannot produce them, it's equally important to allow them some flexibility to use their imaginations and experiences in solving problems and managing their classrooms.

In the past, when a student misbehaved, many schools would issue a consequence to a student, usually outside the classroom. That child would then return to the classroom, and nothing more would be said or done. Restorative justice is about establishing a sense of responsibility to the wider school community. It helps students understand that their behavior can hurt and damage everyone in the classroom, as well as in the larger school community you're trying to build, and that the actions taken by one person can affect everyone. This also lets students know that they need help in a particular behavioral area, just as they might need help in a particular academic area. It's an opportunity for students to be welcomed back into the school community with a clean slate and a chance to start over. If two students get into an argument that disrupts the class, then restorative justice requires that they apologize to the teacher and class after they have first resolved their differences. Restorative justice is about redemption.

MODEL YOUR EXPECTATIONS

Most administrators and principals expect students to come to school knowing how to go to the lunchroom, walk in the halls, and start and finish the day. They expect them to know how to behave.

However, in my eyes, it's a mistake to have that expectation. Many students need to be taught and shown how to behave. In fact, we need to teach behaviors in the same way that we teach math—with clear goals, repetition, and modeling. If you don't provide students with clear guidelines and expectations, they will show up with their own interpretations of how you want things done. Over time, those interpretations become harder and harder to change. On the very first day of the school year, you and your teachers must begin teaching students expectations and behavior for every key area in the school, and every key transition time in the day. As I've said, the smallest things can make a big difference in your school's culture and climate, just as overlooking the little things can lead to big problems.

For example, at some schools, all grade levels enter through the same doors or line up together to go into the auditorium in the morning. This routine often isn't given a second thought. But in certain circumstances, it can be a recipe for chaos and conflict, particularly in struggling schools with histories of behavior challenges. When you're working to truly transform a school, no detail is too small to be considered and planned for in advance.

In the process of considering these details, you will probably find that some teachers struggle with modeling the expected behaviors. Some want to give the kids a manual, have a brief discussion, and leave it at that. It's important for teachers to understand that they have to model behavior each and every day. And for that to happen, administrators also have to model behavior for teachers every day. You have to show teachers the behaviors and responses you expect, not just describe them or list them in a memo. You must prepare them to expect some resistance. Model what you expect and how to respond on the first day of school, so everyone gets it right.

As part of this process, some important questions to ask and answer include:

- What routes will the students take in the morning?
- What grade is going to pass through which door?
- What adults will be stationed in what areas?
- What will students be doing before and after school?
- How is the lunch period going to flow?
- What's the route from the auditorium to the classroom?
- Will everyone take the same staircase, or will grades be split up between different staircases?

These issues must be thought out—and well before school starts. During professional development at the start of the school year, establish and explain positive expectations for every area of the school building, for both staff and students. For example, PBIS recommends that schools create a schoolwide behavior matrix (see Figure 3) based on expectations for those locations you think are most important. Then, in cooperation with your team, you can decide your specific expectations for each location. Give teachers a document explaining your expectations for student behavior in every part of the school, such as the bathrooms, corridors, lunchroom, auditorium, and playground. While you may assume that adults know what proper behavior entails in those areas, you want to make sure that everyone is speaking the same language and that there are no conflicting interpretations about what you mean.

For example, you might decide that students will sit five to a table in the lunchroom. Before the start of the school year, take your staff to the lunchroom and show them exactly how to seat the students and where they should sit. Don't assume anything. Walk them through the lunchroom and model it for them, having them take seats at the tables.

In my lunchroom, I allow only about fifty kids at any one time, and the students eat by grades. This prevents overcrowding and conflicts. When you go to a typical school lunchroom, everyone is moving about. My lunchroom is much more structured with a lot less movement. The student in charge of the garbage can will walk up to each table and the seated students will slide their trays to the end of the table so the assigned student can then empty them. Students are not allowed to just wander about and empty their own trays.

Again, if you have a similar system, model it for teachers. Have them take trays and sit five to a table, while another teacher is in charge of the garbage can. Talk about how students should line up and how trays should be emptied. There has to be a process, and you have to walk your staff through that process. Teachers will then model lunchroom behavior for the students at the beginning of the year. This leaves no room for misinterpretation on anyone's part. Everyone knows exactly what is expected, and you and your staff will send a clear and cohesive message right from the start. Apply this same process of explaining and modeling to the hallways, auditorium, and bathrooms.

Another key time for this modeling and practice happens at the beginning of the year, before the teachers even see their students. Bring teachers outside so you can walk through what the first day is going to look like. I suggest doing this at two locations, such as one place for kindergarten through fourth grade and another for fifth through eighth grade. Teachers should come outside with their signs, paperwork, flyers, or whatever else they will give to parents on the first day of school, and then walk the path they're going to take to their classrooms. That way, a day that is exciting but can also be very chaotic is carefully planned out and leaves less room for disorganization and confusion.

Whenever you talk about procedures, rituals, or traditions, it must be intentional. Each of these practices has to be for a purpose—to make things less hectic and to benefit students. It's all about maximizing your staff's instructional time. If students are running into each other because they don't know which way they're going, or if a class is stuck on the stairs while you're trying to get breakfast served, that creates disorganization, which is not how you want to start your school day.

ESTABLISH CLASSROOM ROUTINES

You will likely struggle to improve your school culture if you have order in the hallways and auditorium but not in your classrooms. For example, each teacher should have a system for students to enter the cloakroom—and for many of the other rituals and routines of a day in the classroom. How do they get everyone's pencils sharpened without squabbles arising? How do they collect papers in an organized way? How do students line up to leave the classroom? If a student comes in late, what is the process for him getting the morning exercise without disrupting the classroom in the process?

Other examples of classroom situations in need of preplanned routines are:

- stopping a classroom activity
- making transitions
- putting away materials
- getting students' attention
- tardy students
- lining up
- exiting the classroom
- turning in incomplete work

To establish and maintain your goals for culture and climate, your entire staff has to be on the same page and be prepared to model every detail.

CREATE A POSITIVE AND WELCOMING CLASSROOM ENVIRONMENT

Another big part of establishing your school's climate is the physical environment. Classrooms should feel like home to students.

With this goal in mind, do everything you can to create a particular sound and feel—a sense of community. Before the school year begins, develop a checklist of items that will be standard in each classroom. Depending on what your budget allows for, you may be able to buy rugs, lamps, and plants. Think about playing soft music over the intercom during passing periods and lunchtime. Each little touch will contribute to the overall feeling you're working to create.

Classrooms should feel like home to students.

Teachers can also use seating arrangements to make their classrooms feel more collaborative and friendly. Suggest that, instead of placing desks in rows, teachers arrange students in groups of three or four where they can congregate and work in small groups. They might also use varied seating arrangements, trapezoid desks, and additions like kidney tables to avoid congestion and obstacles, allowing students to move freely throughout the classroom without running into each other, which helps reduce altercations. The classroom should also be neat and well organized. A cluttered classroom is more likely to encourage misbehavior.

Again, many of your decisions will come back to the same fundamental question: What kind of culture do you want in your school? I've worked in high-poverty schools, where many students come from challenging or chaotic home environments. I can't control that. But I can make sure that when they come to school, they're in a place where they feel welcome, safe, comfortable, and cared for.

I've seen the benefits of this approach firsthand. It takes some students a while to adjust to a new classroom environment, but they end up liking it. In turn, they don't want to miss school. They feel like they are part of something important: A school community where they are valued.

ESTABLISH STUDENT BUY-IN

As you probably know, some teachers tend to be negative controllers. They try to control everything in the classroom, and often use an authoritarian tone: "You do that because I say do it." They often take this approach because they fear completely losing control of their classrooms. But the trade-off is that they usually fail to create buy-in in their classrooms.

Assigning students jobs is one powerful classroom management technique that helps create buy-in. It allows students to have ownership in the classroom and see it as their home away from home. One student may collect papers. Another passes out pencils. A student may help the teacher monitor the bathroom or cloakroom or help pass out breakfast. A teacher can't and shouldn't do it all.

Another way to create buy-in is to use class meetings to make the classroom participatory. These meetings build a sense of community and set a positive tone for the day. Such meetings do not have to be long—five to ten minutes, or ten minutes twice a day, will suffice—but they give students an opportunity to discuss classroom problems or rules or something that happened in the hallway the day before. In some cases, the core issue you're addressing may not even have originated in the classroom or school, but is something that happened in the neighborhood over the weekend and has spilled into the classroom. Still, you have a chance to deal with the situation in a productive way. These meetings can be a chance for students to discuss how they can become better citizens and help their communities.

These meetings should be held regularly, not only when a problem arises. Morning or afternoon meeting times should be listed on the teacher's daily agenda.

These meetings can also be a time when a class recites its creed or affirmation, if that's something you do—or want to implement—at your school. Many schools have a School Creed about respecting one another, the teacher, and the environment, which can do a lot to set the tone for a great day. Teachers may also have other daily classroom routines. One teacher might do a fist bump with everyone in the morning, while in another class teachers and students recite a teambuilding chant together. In yet another class, students might shake their neighbors' hands. All of these little habits and rituals, done as a group, are ways to simply but effectively build community and establish buy-in.

GIVE STUDENTS A VOICE IN THE CLASSROOM RULE-SETTING PROCESS

As a school administrator, assemble various teams in your school to develop your approaches to behavior and academics. This is a lot more effective than a top-down approach where staff is told what to do. The same approach is true of the classroom—students need to have a voice. How do you encourage that voice and incorporate it into your core values? This is a class discussion that you should encourage your teachers to have.

Teachers should be responsible for what the rules are, but students should also participate in establishing these rules so they feel they have some ownership of classroom routines. Otherwise, the rules will seem too restrictive and arbitrary, and students might feel like they're just hearing, "You must do this because I say so."

Students can help establish Rule #1: We will respect Mr. Jackson. They can then have a discussion about the ideas behind the rule. What does respect look like? How can we show it? How does it feel to be respected? After discussing what respect looks like, the students will have a better sense of how they can put Rule #1 into action each and every day. Again, modeling is important. You can't just say to a student "show respect" without modeling what that means.

As you guide teachers to set their classroom rules in partnership with students, advise them not to make too many. In general, five or so should be enough.

In addition to these rules, teachers and students can establish particular ways to communicate with one another. For example, when the teacher is in the process of instructing a lesson, a student might raise two fingers when she needs some tissue. Because the group has discussed this procedure beforehand, everyone knows what's going on. Similarly, raising three fingers might mean that a student needs to use the restroom right away. This type of system can discourage disruption. It can also bring the class together through the process of deciding on these communication procedures.

ALLOW FOR ENTHUSIASM, BUT KNOW WHEN TO SET LIMITS

Routines nurture a sense of community. They are not about stifling energy and enthusiasm. I don't expect every classroom to be silent. A group of students engaged in learning will generate sounds and noises, and that's okay. But there's a difference between a class where teaching and learning is happening and a class that's out of control. The sounds of engagement are distinct from the sounds of disarray.

Of course, there will still be times when students become louder than you want them to be. Advise your staff not to yell over them, because then you'll just end up with a shouting match. Not only will it not bring down the noise levels, but once teachers start using this tactic, they're likely to resort to this approach every time.

Instead, when you want to get students' attention, try standing still and talking in a regular tone of voice. This encourages students to bring their voice levels down to yours. Body language is also a large part of maintaining order. When I walk into a room in my school, the students know right away that Ms. Robbins has arrived. By now they even know my footsteps in the hallway!

When you pay attention to culture and climate in every aspect of your school you might be amazed at what happens. Sometimes students will even hold each other accountable. You might even hear them say things to one another like, "You don't act that way when Ms. Nelson is here. What's the deal?"

PROVIDE ENCOURAGEMENT, AFFIRMATIONS, AND REWARDS

It's important to give authentic praise frequently. For example, at our school, we give tokens to students who are behaving appropriately, which they can spend in the school store. You can put into effect similar programs to encourage the type of behavior you want to maintain. While you can't affirm every positive behavior you see, strive to give praise when it is due. When you see students meeting your expectations, you might say, "Thank you for coming to school every day in your uniform," or "Thank you for walking down the halls with zero noise level," or "You did an excellent job in gym today." Be especially sure to provide positive feedback if you're addressing a class that has had a hard time meeting expectations in the past.

When students don't meet your expectations, you can use "Do It Again" to reach an appropriate level of behavior. Let's say a teacher has a system of collecting papers specifying that everyone passes their papers to the right and the last person puts them into a stack on the teacher's desk. The teacher allows three minutes for this. If it doesn't happen in three minutes, the teacher will do it again until the students can accomplish that goal as a group. When the goal is met, the teacher praises them: "You guys did a fantastic job. You kept trying until you got it right, and I appreciate the work that you've done."

Through authentic praise, you can create a common language in your school. And the language you use as an administrator will become the language of a new, more positive school culture. For instance, you or your dean might greet the students one morning by saying, "We're going to make it a great day. Happy Thursday to everyone. You look good in your uniforms. Thank you for coming to school wearing them every day. Let's remember that in our halls there's a zero noise level."

Similarly, when students pass teachers who are not their own, those teachers might say, "Wow, you guys look good," or "Ms. McCarthy, I didn't even know your class was in the hallway. Excellent job!" Or: "You students are so well behaved, even though you don't have your regular teacher today." As a visionary leader, the tone you set filters down to every aspect of your school.

As important as it is to support your students, it's also wise not to give praise when it is not due, because then, over time, praise ceases to mean anything. In my school, sometimes I walk by a classroom and a student will say, "Ms. Robbins, can you give us a compliment?" because the teacher has promised the class something if they get enough compliments. In that case I'll say, "You look good, but not this time." They have to earn it.

In addition to authentic praise, you can do a number of other things to show students that they're meeting expectations. For instance, you could give three monthly schoolwide rewards—one for Student of the Month, one for straight As, and one for perfect attendance.

The Student of the Month is chosen for each class by the teacher, and it is not based on academics, but on behavior and good effort. Tell your teachers that you don't want to see them choose the same child each month. For some students, a C is the best they can do right now. Or maybe a student has had a good couple of days or a good couple of weeks and deserves recognition for that. These are not the straight-A students, but they shouldn't be overlooked. As awards you could give out certificates, snacks, or other small

> *Through authentic praise, you can create a common language in your school.*

prizes. Another incentive you could offer to Students of the Month is the chance to take a picture with you, which is then posted on a bulletin board in a hallway or other common area.

Along these same lines, you could award something every month for students who earn straight As, and for those who achieve perfect attendance. You might also have quarterly awards for academics, such as Honor Roll and Principal's Scholars.

On top of these schoolwide recognitions, encourage your teachers to also give rewards and provide celebrations—when earned and appropriate—in their individuals classrooms. These can range from dance parties to popcorn and movie breaks. I've found that it's particularly helpful to provide at least small rewards and incentives on a regular basis, such as every two weeks.

PROMOTE "GOOD NOTES" AND POSITIVE PHONE CALLS

Just as you have norms in your school to address misbehavior, you will also have norms that reward positive behavior. In keeping with this, make sure that your teachers notify parents whenever their students have done a good job.

"Good Notes" is a reward approach that I developed. It's a template note that teachers can send home: "Your child had a great day in art" or "Your child had a great day today in math. I noticed some improvement. Keep up the good work." Students love taking these notes home to post on the refrigerator, as recognition that they're doing well. (You and your teachers can craft your own original "Good Notes" or look online for examples. Pinterest is a great source for inspiration and ideas.)

It sounds simple, but a history of a brief positive note will go a long way when James starts slacking off in reading and you have to bring up improvement issues with his parent. By emphasizing the positive before the negative, you help build parent-teacher and school-home relationships. This is especially crucial if you're trying to change the community's perception of a struggling school.

Positive phone calls are another way to recognize students—not just calling when a student has had a fight or has been disruptive, but when he's had a good day by being really engaged in classroom instruction. If you do that more often than the other phone calls, you'll get a better response from parents when you need to bring up behavior problems.

Stay Persistent, But Be Willing to Seek Other Methods

The approaches and routines I've described in this chapter will help 95 per-cent of the student body. For the other 5 percent, in which most students will have IEPs, it may be mandated that each student see a social worker. These social workers are your teammates in getting additional services for students and families who need more help. Making the best use of your counseling and social work staff is discussed in greater detail in Chapter Six.

Room for Reflection

CULTURE AND CLIMATE

- Are you satisfied with your school's culture and climate? Where do you see room for improvement?

- What changes will you make in your approach to discipline after reading this chapter?

- What specific tools do you want to implement as you work to improve your school's culture and climate?

- List three goals for improving your school's culture and climate in the coming school year or term. How will you achieve them?

DISCIPLINE REFERRAL FORM

Student Name _____

IEP? ☐ Yes ☐ No   Repeat Offense? ☐ Yes ☐ No

Room _____   Grade _____

Time _____   Date _____

Referred by _____

Location: ☐ Classroom   ☐ Cafeteria   ☐ Hallway   ☐ Bathroom   ☐ Assembly
          ☐ Playground   ☐ Arrival/Dismissal   ☐ Other _____

CLASSROOM ISSUES

☐ Chewing gum or eating candy*
☐ Not having supplies*
These infractions should never become office issues

☐ Tardiness or absence**
**Follow school attendance procedures*

☐ Excessive talking
☐ Throwing small objects
☐ Sleeping in class
☐ Minor stealing
☐ Working off-task
☐ Minor altercation (running, pushing, or horseplay)
☐ Being disruptive in classroom or hallway
☐ Being disrespectful
☐ Refusing to follow directions
☐ Cheating or plagiarizing
☐ Profanity
☐ Use of a cell phone or other electronic device (*single use*)
☐ Other_____
*Submit office referral form **after any third** violation.*

OFFICE ISSUES

☐ Skipping class or leaving school (truancy)
☐ Writing notes that contain lewd or threatening content
☐ Fighting
☐ Having weapons at school
☐ Possession or being under the influence of tobacco or drugs
☐ Property damage
☐ Theft
☐ Bullying, intimidation/physical threatening
☐ Sexual harassment
☐ Defiance of authority/gross disrespect/insubordination
☐ Gang-related activity
☐ Use of a cell phone or other electronic device (*multiple uses*)
☐ Excessive profanity or profanity directed at adults
☐ Threats against staff or students
☐ Other_____

☐ **STAFF/TEACHER ACTION:**	☐ **OFFICE ACTION:**
☐ Verbal warning	☐ Verbal reprimand
☐ Student conference	☐ Parent telephone contact
☐ Parent telephone contact	☐ Parent meeting
☐ Teacher-issued consequence	☐ Loss of privileges
☐ Parent meeting	☐ Detention/community service
☐ Student behavior contract	☐ In-school suspension
☐ Detention	☐ Suspension: # of days: _____
☐ Community service	☐ Other _____

Teacher or staff description of behavior:

_____

_____

_____

_____

_____

_____

_____

_____

_____

Teacher or staff description of action taken:

_____

_____

_____

_____

_____

_____

_____

_____

_____

Administrator's Signature _____

Date _____

CHAPTER FIVE
Professional Development—Creating and Sustaining a Proficient Learning Community

One good teacher has the power to push a student forward in dramatic ways. We've all seen the impact an amazing teacher can have on children's lives. On the flip side, however, poor instruction has the potential to set back a child for many years. As a visionary leader, part of your job is to help all teachers be their best. If your staff includes teachers who have challenges in the classroom, how do you support them? How do you help transform a teacher who is struggling? How do you help improve a teacher's craft?

You can do all of this through professional development (PD), the improvement of skills and knowledge, which may involve coaching and reflection to help teachers see their classrooms and students in new and different ways. Teachers who engage in ongoing, purposeful professional development will affect the most change and improvement in students' lives. Without quality, in-depth, and ongoing PD, it will be harder for you to transform teaching and raise student achievement.

Most professionals, in a wide variety of fields, engage in professional development to maintain and improve their professional competence, enhance career progression, keep abreast of new technology and practice, and comply with professional regulations. Why shouldn't teachers also engage in lifelong professional improvement? Why shouldn't teachers consider PD to be their professional obligation in order to improve their craft and continue to be relevant and competent in their fields? Surely teachers are as important as any profession in our society.

Professional development can take many forms, including consultation, coaching, communities of practice and study, mentoring, reflective supervision, and technical assistance. As an administrator and instructional leader, you are an integral part of the success of any professional development program. It is your responsibility to establish and implement a transformative PD program in your school.

Overview of the Professional Development Process

I created the chart shown in Figure 5 to help guide my staff in professional development on a schoolwide basis. You and your staff can enter this chart or process at any point. Different situations may demand that you start at different points in this process.

While you will often start with a goal, in some instances you may have to first assess and reflect to determine your goal and the plan of action to reach it. Perhaps you've gotten your assessment data back, and you can see that students need help improving their math scores. What, then, will be your PD goals to improve those scores? What will be the next step in coaching and mentoring teachers around math instruction? The goals in this case flow from the assessment and subsequent reflection.

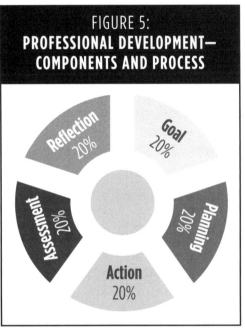

FIGURE 5:
PROFESSIONAL DEVELOPMENT—
COMPONENTS AND PROCESS

Reflection 20%

Goal 20%

Assessment 20%

Planning 20%

Action 20%

In other situations, such as at the start of school year, you can start with broad goals around attendance and discipline, and then do assessment and reflection to determine how to reach those goals. Starting with a goal is usually the best approach when you want to establish guidelines for discipline and behavior. You know your goals for student behavior and you don't need to spend a lot of time reflecting on them. Instead, you need to put a plan into action as soon as school starts, not three months into the term.

The chart in Figure 5 applies to schoolwide issues, but it can also be used to address specific classrooms and teachers. Suppose your fourth-grade teacher is struggling with managing her students. How do you assess what's causing this problem? What is the goal for this teacher? What is the plan to help her reach that goal? What specific actions will she take as part of that plan, and how will you support her in the process?

At the start of the year, ask your teachers to set a few individual goals to improve their teaching and learning. Then hold a one-on-one meeting with each teacher to discuss a plan to help him or her achieve those goals. Following these initial meetings, it's important to check in during the year to see how those goals are being met. In doing this, don't forget about the good teachers who are already doing everything you need and want. As with students, we tend to give attention to those teachers who are showing red flags, while sometimes ignoring those who are doing well. It's important to be mindful of this issue in conducting professional development.

Using the information in Figure 5, ask yourself questions at each stage of the process to help form your professional development strategies, both on a schoolwide basis and for individual teachers.

Let's look at math and science instruction as an example.

1. Goal: Improve math and science instruction in sixth grade
- According to the data and/or observation, where are we today on this issue?
- Where do we want to be?
- When do we want to be there?
- What are the essential skills I want my staff to know and master to achieve this goal?

2. Plan
- What are the logistics (who, what, when, where)?
- What materials will we need?
- What training will take place?
- How can we make this training meaningful and relevant for staff?
- Which students will we focus on most? Why?

3. Action
- What variety of methods will we use over time to provide and sustain new learning?
- What method will make the biggest difference as we maximize student learning?

4. Assessment
- What data will we collect?
- How will we collect that data?
- What will be the frequency of data collection?
- Who will gather the data?
- What other evidence will be collected?
- How will the staff know the overall plan is working?

5. Reflection
- What positive impact has this had on student learning and student engagement?
- Based on results, what strategic changes are needed?
- How is this getting us closer to our goal?
- What can be celebrated?
- How can we share this with others, including parents, students, the school board, community members, and other stakeholders?
- How will we continue to present this information to others?

Eleven Core Principles and Practices of Professional Development

In my experience, even when you hire a really great teacher who has everything you want, on that first day in the classroom, she may not know where to start. All she knows for sure is that on Monday morning she's going to have twenty-seven kids calling her the teacher.

You may have hired someone with the right character and chemistry, and she may be displaying all the things you want in a teacher. You know you have a competent person in front of you, but she still needs guidance. She may be creative and able to take a lesson and run with it, but your role is to help shape and develop and augment those skills. She may be unprepared for the great variety of ability levels in one classroom but willing and able to learn new strategies and teaching practices. Teachers have to be nurtured and cultivated. It takes a special kind of leader to do that. You can use the following principles and practices to craft professional development that will bring your staff to a higher level as teachers and help your school reach its goals.

#1: IDENTIFY NEEDS AND DESIGN PD TO MATCH THOSE NEEDS

Identifying gaps in teaching practice starts with going into classrooms. This is the first step in developing professional learning dialogues with teachers. As described earlier, you'll be out of your office during the majority of your day, observing, assessing, and giving feedback to teachers.

While observing teachers, look for patterns. If you see the same problem in four or five classrooms, that's a red flag. The problem is not an isolated one, but an issue that needs to be addressed with a grade level, with a cluster, or with everyone.

The foundation of successful professional development is data. In coaching an individual teacher, you're looking for those patterns or red flags that are also associated with some type of data. For example, you may have a teacher who is turning in an enormous number of misconduct reports for his students. Take a look at where the misbehavior is happening and which students are being referred. Are they the same students? Is it happening at the same time of day? By looking at different pieces of data, you can begin to isolate the problem and then provide the teacher or teachers in question with professional development around classroom management.

Or the data could point to an academic problem centered around a specific skill. A teacher's grade book might indicate that many students are failing a particular assignment or exam. When you see a pattern like that develop, you might want to have a conversation with the teacher about assessments or reteaching a particular skill. You will focus professional development around whatever that teacher needs.

When you're conducting your classroom observations, you'll always want to have some academic data in the back of your mind about the particular teacher and classroom you're visiting. The two main sources of this data are likely to be student grades and the most recent high-stakes assessment (such as the latest Common Core assessment). You could also review data on behavior referrals or classroom management issues.

You may want to routinely conduct grade book audits—on a weekly basis, for example—in which you look at the percentage of students in a class who have not mastered a certain skill. Are the students making progress with what the teacher is currently teaching? Based on these audits and other assessment data, if you see patterns or data that concern you, have a conversation with the teacher. Ask questions like: "Why are students not mastering this skill? Have you taken some time to reflect on how you're going to reteach it? What's your plan for doing that? Do you need to look at some different materials? Do you need to target certain students?"

Again, this is the type of difficult conversation administrators need to have. If you let these conversations fall by the wayside, gaps in academic performance will get bigger and bigger. But make sure that these conversations are always backed by data.

#2: HELP TEACHERS CONNECT CURRICULUM WITH STANDARDS AND LEARNING OUTCOMES

As the instructional leader, you must help teachers connect the curriculum with the learning standards and outcomes you want them to achieve. A major way of doing that is through regular data assessment.

Every two weeks, hold a meeting to look at data from each of your grades, clusters, or other organizational units. Require teachers to come to these meetings with academic data they've gathered in their classrooms. I recommend looking at teachers' grade books, where you'll be able to see information on class averages, class mastery, the students who achieved passing grades, and those who failed. Teachers should also bring assignments and the assessments given, which might include mini-assessments such as Do Nows or Exit Tickets, or through other methods. (For more information on Do Nows and Exit Tickets, see Chapter Six.)

In addition to reviewing classroom data, frequently review your schoolwide data, including numbers on discipline and attendance. You might want to review it yourself every week, and then review it with staff every two weeks. At these biweekly meetings, you could distribute a bulletin communicating the big picture to your staff. By keeping this data in front of you at all times and reviewing it frequently and systematically, you and your team will have a clear vision of what's working well and what changes need to be made.

Measurement systems can shed light on areas of achievement and also on areas where you need further growth. For instance, if you systematically track how many misconduct referrals a teacher has, that data will allow you to see where the teacher is having the most difficulty—in the lunchroom, in the corridors, during transition times, or in some other area. Measuring points for concern will help reinforce what's most important to your team and your school. In turn, that enables you to help a teacher in specific targeted areas, while at the same time acknowledging their achievements and growth.

Perhaps your goal in the previous year was 50 percent of students reading at or above grade level, and this year you've set a new goal of 60 percent. The data will tell you where you are with that goal and what you need to do next. Staff will be aware of all reading, math, and science statistics, so everyone is clear about your goals and the progress being made toward achieving them. And that information is posted on the walls of the school.

It takes a special kind of leader to nurture and cultivate teachers.

One of the biggest challenges in professional development—and especially around data—concerns veteran teachers. Many of them are very knowledgeable, but it can be difficult to get them to change some of their practices, based on the students in front of them. In particular, it's sometimes tough to convince these teachers to really dig into the data, because in years past it wasn't as important as it is today. I know when I was starting out as a teacher, data wasn't as much in the forefront as it is now. Be mindful of this when conducting PD with veteran teachers. You may need to tailor certain professional development with the goal of helping some teachers see the value of data and embrace good methods of both collecting and analyzing it.

#3: DEMONSTRATE HOW COACHING CAN IMPROVE INSTRUCTION

Once you begin PD, you have to make it clear to staff that you and the Instructional Leadership Team are going to be coming into classrooms to coach. It has to be clear that this isn't about "catching" teachers at their worst moments or doing something wrong. Coaching is about supporting, trusting, and respecting teachers. Teachers have to feel comfortable with coaching in order for transparent and truthful dialogue to take place. They can't feel guarded or defensive.

Still, coaching can be stressful for some teachers, especially if they previously taught in schools where they could shut their classroom doors and do it their way without feedback or close supervision. It's often stressful to hear critical feedback, but that feedback must nevertheless be delivered. As an administrator working to improve your school, you need to initiate and lead conversations about what the coaching model is going to look like, what its goals will be, and how it will improve instruction and student outcomes.

One way to structure coaching is to have coaches assigned to specific grade levels or groups. For example, I have three coaches assisting me: one each for the primary, middle, and upper grades. Through regular PD meetings, these coaches will keep you informed about who is being coached, in what areas, and with what results.

Coaches support teachers by giving detailed suggestions about classroom issues. As an example, I once had a kindergarten teacher who was struggling to manage her classroom and build relationships with students. This was partly because she had missed two weeks of classes due to personal issues. During her absence, the class fell apart. Her initial hard work started to disappear because students needed the structure and consistency of her presence.

When she returned she received intense, real-time coaching. She wore a headphone set and an earbud, while a coach observing from the back of the room gave her feedback and instructions. The coach tried to stay a step ahead, sharing observations as the teacher delivered the lesson or made transitions in the classroom. The coach might say, "I noticed you weren't calling on students in the back of the room. You only interacted with four or five students who sat in the front, and those were the students who raised their hands. You didn't spread yourself around to facilitate the entire classroom." The next step is for the coach to make specific suggestions. "Move to the right side of the classroom, stand behind John, and give a countdown for him to make a transition." The teacher was very open to receiving this type of coaching, and as a result, she not only kept her job, but also became a stronger classroom manager.

For more detailed information on coaching techniques and approaches, see Chapter Six.

#4: MAKE ONGOING PROFESSIONAL CONVERSATIONS PART OF THE FABRIC OF SCHOOL LIFE

Professional conversations are the fabric of any teaching community. That means you're in a dialogue with teachers about everything you do schoolwide: "How do we become better as a staff? As a school? How do we get students to become better? What do we most need to work on?"

Every time you meet as a staff, you will likely wrestle with these questions in multiple ways. Provide books and articles as springboards for conversation. Use your classroom observations to initiate discussion and reflection. Encourage your staff to work together, brainstorm, and make use of everyone's different perspectives and expertise. And always make it clear that your school is not one where teachers can close their classroom doors and work alone. Foster an environment that is open and transparent.

PREPARE TEACHERS TO ACCEPT FEEDBACK

An essential part of professional conversations is the willingness to accept honest, constructive feedback. You might find, for instance, that you have a teacher with a high number of unsatisfactory remarks around Charlotte Danielson's Domain 1, Planning and Preparation. In response, you could sit down with that teacher to walk her through a PD plan, and set up a system of meeting every week to discuss her lesson plans with you.

When you have these meetings, talk about the many facets of Danielson's Domain 1. For instance, it requires that teachers demonstrate their knowledge of content standards, instructional strategies, and prerequisite learning. They must understand what needs to be done to build up to a particular lesson and know that lesson's relationship with other content areas. They need to select learning objectives, decide on a sequence of learning, be clear on how they will build student mastery, and describe the types of learning that will be incorporated into the lesson. They need to design student assessments, making sure that these assessments align with lesson objectives and that expectations for student performance are clearly identified. They need to demonstrate knowledge of their students' backgrounds, abilities, learning styles, individual needs, and interests. Furthermore, Domain 1 requires that teachers design coherent instruction and materials, that they understand pacing, and that they are clear on how they will differentiate support for their students.

As you explore these requirements, make them relevant to the lesson plan in front of you. Help the teacher see how her plans do and do not fulfill those requirements and how she can improve her lesson plans to better meet your expectations.

A teacher you meet with in this way might be surprised by the intensity of the PD plan. She may ask, "Are we really going to be doing this every week?" Be clear about what you expect to see. You might respond, "Yes, until I can see from your lesson plans that you've got it and that your plans are much more detailed and specific. Then we can taper off and perhaps move to another part of teaching practice."

The frequency of your one-on-one meetings with teachers will be based on the amount of progress you see happening. You may have to meet with some teachers once a week or twice a month throughout the school year. Whatever schedule you set, these professional conversations must become a part of the regular protocol of your Instructional Leadership Team or other core group.

In addition to being the focus of many one-on-one meetings, PD conversations should be part of larger staff meetings. Your teachers need to get used to seeing professional development as an everyday activity, not just something that is relegated to official PD meetings.

Of course, you won't be in every meeting your staff has. And in some cases, it will not be enough to simply request that teachers have a professional conversation or an academic dialogue when they gather. You may need give direction for addressing specific academic problems and achieving specific goals, especially during meetings you cannot attend.

FROM THE PRINCIPAL'S DESK

A challenge I once faced with my staff was that their grade-level meetings weren't very productive when I wasn't present, and they didn't focus on PD conversations. To address this issue, I introduced a PD feedback form for teachers to fill out in all meetings. I also provided goals and assignments for certain meetings. For instance, I introduced a PD assignment called Depth of Knowledge, which helps teachers align student learning with different levels of rigor. I told them I wanted all of our student assignments to be at levels three or four, which are the most rigorous and challenging. To facilitate reaching this goal, I gave teachers topics to discuss during their grade-level meetings. I wanted them to give feedback to each other and ask questions: "How did you develop this assignment? Where did you get the idea? Let me help you make this stronger." And to make sure these conversations were taking place, I required teachers to fill out the PD feedback forms and turn them in to me. Even when I am at a meeting, I ask teachers to fill out the form. Some teachers may write down perspectives that they didn't want to mention in the meeting or record questions that weren't asked but that you can follow up on. In addition, filling out this form is simply a good reminder to stay on task and focused.

BE RECEPTIVE TO FEEDBACK FROM TEACHERS

Effective PD is founded on the idea that you must be willing to give direct and honest feedback to your teachers, and your teachers must be willing to accept it. This requires a great degree of trust between staff members and administration. One way to build that trust is to make feedback a two-way street. An administrator should also be willing to accept constructive feedback.

At the start of the year I do something called Word Café. I set up four or five huge posters in the school corridor where everyone can see them, and at the top I write various headings like, "I like it when my principal . . ." and "My principal makes me feel . . ." Teachers use sticky notes to complete these sentences. It's done anonymously, and it gives me a sense of how my staff is viewing me and the progress of some of our programs.

I also use anonymous surveys midyear and at the end of the year to assess my staff's honest view of how we're progressing. Transparent, two-way feedback is essential in building mutual trust. If your teachers know that you are willing to accept their feedback, they will be more willing to accept yours.

#5: SHOW TEACHERS HOW TO EMBED ONGOING ASSESSMENT INTO ALL TEACHING

Another element of a strong PD program is evaluating your teachers' ability to assess learning in the classroom and teaching them a variety of strategies for doing so. You also need to show them how to use that assessment—before, during, and after instruction—to inform practice.

Naturally, how teachers plan and conduct lessons will be driven, in part, by meeting state standards. And to determine whether students are meeting those standards, your school will conduct a variety of assessments several times a year. (For more information on assessment, see Chapter Seven.)

But you can also teach your staff other ways of assessing whether students are learning. For instance, Do Nows and Exit Tickets (described in more detail in Chapter Six) are mini-assessments that give teachers a quick snapshot of who got the lesson and who might need extra attention in a small group. These assessments can take place before, during, and after a lesson.

Another assessment strategy teachers often overlook is "wait time" within instruction. Sometimes teachers want to get quick responses from students during a lesson. But not all students will think as fast as you're teaching. If you give them some wait time, or call on someone else and come back, that gives the quieter students a chance to formalize their thoughts and give you an answer.

I suggest requiring teachers to conduct some type of assessment every week, in addition to two in-class assignments and one homework assignment. These must be recorded in their grade books, and must be presented in a way that allows you to check on them easily. For instance, a system of color-coding can help make data quick and easy to interpret.

You may encounter some pushback on a requirement like this, especially from teachers who are responsible for two or more content areas. In some cases, you can allow for assignments to be integrated, such as combining social studies and language arts in the same assignment. But in reading and math, for purposes of key data collection, I don't recommend offering any exceptions to two in-class assignments, one assessment, and one homework assignment each week.

Offer your teachers the flexibility to create their own assessments, but keep an eye on the quality of data these assessments produce. Also evaluate whether the assessments are clearly and closely aligned to standards. If you find that some teachers struggle to create the high-quality assessments that must be given on a weekly basis, you may need to look for programs that will help them do it. For instance, the software package Measuring Up Insight generates assignments and assessments focused on the Common Core for second through eighth grade.

#6: MAKE EFFECTIVE LESSON PLANS THE FOUNDATION OF INTENTIONAL INSTRUCTION

Talk frequently and consistently with teachers about being intentional and deliberate in their practice. You can gauge a teacher's level of intention by his lesson plans. If the plans are too broad, he isn't being deliberate and intentional enough. But when he can script out his lessons in detail, then you'll know he's got it.

Data is hugely important to intentional teaching, but the planning process is just as critical. If you don't plan well, data alone will not help you get great results. Good planning takes data into account and develops a method, in the form of a lesson plan, to put that data to effective use. You don't need to ask teachers to give you a fully scripted plan for every single lesson, because that's a lot of work—both for them and for you. But teachers *do* need to plan almost every instructional moment of their days, so that their work yields the results your school is striving for.

So many unexpected things can happen during a teacher's day. But if a teacher isn't ready for the unexpected, and hasn't planned for how she can handle it, she'll lose instructional time, which is unacceptable. My teachers tell me they now spend most of their weekends doing their lesson plans, whereas in the past they would spend no more than an hour developing them. Teachers simply can't afford to just throw their lessons together. If they do, the lack of preparation will definitely show.

You may be wondering: Isn't burnout an issue? When do teachers have time to rest?

As an administrator, you have to demand high standards while also being supportive of teachers. There are ups and downs during the school year, and for the most part teachers have a good sense of the year's rhythms: when a lot will be demanded of them and when they can step back and rest a bit. Be mindful of these peaks and valleys. Keep the culture and climate positive, and do what you can throughout the year to let your staff know that you support them during the rough times. Provide teachers with baskets of fruit and other snacks. Give them words of encouragement and put appreciative notes in their mailboxes. In your weekly bulletins, acknowledge their efforts: "This is a time of year when we don't have a break. I know it isn't easy, but you're not in this by yourself!"

Even at the most difficult times, however, you cannot compromise on lesson plans. If you like, you can offer your teachers a lesson plan template they can work from. However, you don't need to insist that every teacher work from exactly the same format, as long as the quality of their plans meets your standards. Give them detailed information about what you expect to see in their lesson plan, and make sure they include it.

A good lesson plan asks and answers this essential question: "What are you expecting students to know and be able to do in this week's lesson?" Ask to see the optimal learning model in teachers' lesson plans, which tells you what the teacher is going to do (I Do), what the teacher is going to do together with the class (We Do), and then what the teacher is going to have the students do (You Do). How will the teacher craft instruction around vocabulary? What small-group interventions will the teacher use? What is assessment going to look like? Will technology be integrated into the lesson plan? What types of materials will be used?

To give your teachers additional guidance on improving their lesson plans, you can use a Lesson Plan Feedback Form, which you'll find as a reproducible on page 120.

Because lesson plans are so crucial, I have included an example of a good general lesson plan in Figure 6 on pages 106–107, and a small-group instruction plan in Figure 7 on page 108. This level of detail is what you're looking for when you review weekly plans. If you find that some teachers need extra guidance in creating their plans, you can direct them to examples from DePaul University, which I have found helpful in my work (teacher.depaul.edu/Lesson_Planning_Structures_and_Guides.html).

#7: CREATE A RESPECTFUL SPACE FOR QUESTIONING TEACHING PRACTICES

At the start of the year, talk with your staff about the boundaries needed to create a productive professional learning community. Establishing respectful boundaries is crucial for a successful PD program. When people are receiving and exchanging constructive feedback and criticism, proper boundaries make successful communication possible.

As you set up these boundaries, agree on group norms ensuring that you are respectful toward one another and provide a safe haven for everyone. Acknowledge that you won't always have the same opinions, but that you'll listen to each other and be respectful of each other's ideas.

Your group norms should also require that all members of the team actively participate in professional development meetings and conversations. Teachers can be an unreceptive audience sometimes, especially if they don't expect to get anything out of a meeting or presentation. In addition, depending on your school's history and its past approach to professional development, some teachers may not be accustomed to getting quality PD. They might have a tendency to start grading papers during meetings, talk with each other, or simply refuse to participate.

So, at the beginning of the year and your PD program, ask staff to keep an open mind and interact with others about what the facilitator has asked them to discuss. Let teachers know that they'll need to be able to take what they learn from PD back to the classrooms and use it with their students.

FIGURE 6: SAMPLE FIFTH-GRADE SCIENCE LESSON PLAN

Topic: Growth and Survival

Focus question of the week: "What is the water cycle?"

Key academic vocabulary: water cycle, evaporation, condensation

This week's reading: "Water in the Air," "The Water Cycle," "Energy in the Water Cycle"

This week's writing: Three explanatory journal entries (one discussing each reading), plus a report summarizing and synthesizing the week's content and including all of the key academic vocabulary

Learning habits aligned with Common Core: Answer questions with *evidence* (CCR1); *Infer meanings* of words from context (CCR4)

This week's Common Core Standards emphasized: CCSSR1; CCSSR2; CCSSR5; CCSSR7

MONDAY Preview, Model, Interest	TUESDAY Model and Guide	WEDNESDAY Go Deeper	THURSDAY Assess and Clarify	FRIDAY Fix and Finish Up
Objective: To describe how the water cycle works.	**Objective:** To observe water in three different forms.	**Objective:** To learn more about the water cycle.	**Objective:** To assess students' knowledge of lesson content.	**Objective:** To synthesize the week's learning and determine each student's level of independent competence.
Teacher (I Do) Ask a volunteer to read I WILL KNOW at the top of page 258. Help students connect these ideas to their world.	**Teacher (I Do)** Call students' attention to ENVISION IT at the top of page 259. Read the ENVISION IT question with students. Discuss with students what form of water is shown on this page.	**Teacher (I Do)** Tell students that we will be reading about how the water cycle works. Have them look at the diagram on pages 260 and 261.	**Students (You Do)** *Formative Assessment* Give students an assessment on this week's lesson.	**Teacher (I Do) and Teacher/Students (We Do)** Review the week's subject matter. Use a graphic organizer to clarify ideas and relevant information and discuss it with students.
Teacher/Students (We Do) With students, read "Water in the Air" on page 258. Work with them to complete the sequence activity on the same page.	**Teacher/Students (We Do)** While preparing to perform our activity, discuss with students that we can often see water change form right in front of our eyes.	**Teacher/Students (We Do)** Read "The Water Cycle" on pages 260 and 261. After reading, ask the following questions: • Where do you think the water cycle begins? • How might pesticides and fertilizers on land become a problem in an ocean ecosystem?	**Teacher (I Do)** Clarify topics based on how students respond to the assessment. Those students who need extra support on lesson content based on the assessment results will do the lesson Check assignment.	Students needing support will be retaught, using additional differentiation as needed.

Students (You Do)
Students will complete the "My Planet Diary" assignment.

Exit-Check for Understanding
Have students write 50–100 words about what they learned about the water cycle and how that information connects to knowledge they already had.

HOMEWORK
Got It #8

Small-Group Instruction and Guided Reading Groups
–All students will participate in activities, observations, and recording in notebooks.
–Based on needs and strengths, students will participate in Cooperative Learning Groups, collaborative small-group conversations, and/or Question-Answer Relationship small-group discussion.
–Special needs students may need more support with recording in notebooks and explanation of concepts.

Students (You Do)
Students will perform the activity, "How does water change?" on page 262. Students will try to observe water in three different forms.

Exit-Check for Understanding
Have students draw the water cycle and forms of water.

HOMEWORK
Got It #9

How will the use of a graphic organizer be incorporated?
Students will observe, list, record, and sketch their observations through graphic organizers such as graphs and charts.

Students (You Do)
Have students complete the water cycle diagram on pages 260 and 261.

Exit-Check for Understanding
Have students work in small groups to compose three questions about the water cycle. Have each group pose their questions to another group.

HOMEWORK
Finish pages 262–263.

Exit-Check for Understanding
Ask students to think about the way they answered the BIG QUESTION when the chapter was first introduced. Challenge them to think about how they would change their answer now that they know more about the water cycle.

HOMEWORK
Complete assignment on page 263.

Students (You Do)
Students who do meet the week's expectations and objectives will advance to complete independent projects which may include:
• writing a booklet about the topic
• making a display about the topic
• giving a presentation on the topic

Synthesis and Conclusion
What did we learn about science this week?
What did we learn about learning science?

HOMEWORK
Complete reading on pages 265–270 to prepare for next week's lesson.

Please submit your assessment with these plans.

Used by permission. Original model developed by Barbara Radner, Ph.D. (teacher.depaul.edu).

FIGURE 7: SAMPLE SMALL-GROUP INSTRUCTION LESSON PLAN, FIFTH-GRADE LANGUAGE ARTS

Teacher: Ms. Clark **Room:** 310 **Grade:** 5 **Date:** April 20–24

Data-to-Instruction Framework Template	
Content Area	English Language Arts
Topic/Standard	**RI.4.4** Ask and answer questions to help determine or clarify the meaning of words and phrases in a text.
Performance Goals	**Primary Performance Goal:** Use and understand context clues and references in informational text. **Secondary Performance Goal:** Use context to determine the meaning of domain-specific words or phrases in informational text.

Score Range	Student Groups	Skills from Selected Learning Statements	Student Activities	Instructional Strategies	Assessment
Lower Range: 150–180 Frequency: Daily **2x** 3x	M. Esparza T. Lewis-Johnson M. Rayas A. White D. Hunter T. Johnson A. Jordon J. McFarland T. Henderson K. Scott	Using context clues to determine or clarify the meaning of words and phrases in informational text. **Key vocabulary:** nonfiction clue	**Small-group learning target:** Students will be able to find the meaning of the words or phrases in a text by using context clues. Students will be reading "Mother Nature Recycles" and answering questions to determine the meaning of words.	Small-group work and use of at least one of the following: ___ Manipulatives _X_ Graphic organizer _X_ Pre-teaching _X_ Simplifying/Rephrasing ___ Repetition ___ Flashcards _X_ Visual and verbal cues _X_ Other, please specify: Read the story to them and then together	Students will receive a passage with 1 to 3 questions to determine the meaning of words in text using context clues in informational text.
Middle Range: 195–200 Frequency: Daily 2x **3x**	J. McGlothin C. Mitchell E. Lucas B. Summer D. Bell C. Ortiz C. Armstrong S. Piggott A. Bulter N. Castillo K. Gant	Using context clues to determine or clarify the meaning of words and phrases in informational text. **Key vocabulary:** nonfiction clue	**Small-group learning target:** Students will be able to find the meaning of the words or phrases in a text by using context clues. Students will be reading "Ever Wonder" and answering questions to determine the meaning of words.	Small-group work and use of at least one of the following: ___ Manipulatives _X_ Graphic organizer _X_ Pre-teaching _X_ Simplifying/Rephrasing ___ Repetition ___ Flashcards _X_ Visual and verbal cues ___ Other, please specify:	Students will receive a passage with 1 to 6 questions to determine the meaning of words in a text using context clues in informational text.
Top Range: 200–222 Frequency: Daily **2x** 3x	D. Bass M. Martin K. Mason D. Morrow J. Camacho T. Su'aMorrison	Using context clues to determine or clarify the meaning of words and phrases in informational text. **Key vocabulary:** nonfiction clue	**Small-group learning target:** Students will be able to find the meaning of the words or phrases in a text by using context clues. Students will be reading "The Porcupine" and answering questions to determine the meaning of words.	Small-group work and use of at least one of the following: ___ Manipulatives ___ Graphic organizer _X_ Pre-teaching ___ Simplifying/Rephrasing ___ Repetition ___ Flashcards _X_ Visual and verbal cues ___ Other, please specify:	Students will receive a passage with 1 to 8 questions to determine the meaning of words in a text using context clues in informational text.

Adapted from materials created by the Northwest Education Association (nwea.org).

Once you've established boundaries and norms for your PD community, you'll be better able to prepare teachers for the honest critiques that are part of effective PD. Teachers must be willing to question their own practices, and they must be open to others doing so. They need to be prepared to ask and answer the questions, "Am I on the right track? How can I do this better? How can my administrators support me? What are other resources I can pull from?"

This process can be intimidating or scary for some teachers at first, but it's essential. You can take steps to make your staff more comfortable with the idea.

One simple technique is "Wows and Wonders." When you observe a teacher, leave him or her with little notes, called "Wows" and "Wonders." For example, "Wow, the student engagement is really high in this class!" and, "I wonder why you only took questions from three students in the front of the classroom." These notes can be a first small step in acclimating teachers to accepting more challenging questions (as well as encouragement) about what they do. Once teachers become accustomed to receiving constructive criticism along with encouragement, you start to build trust. It then becomes less unsettling for someone to come into their classrooms and ask questions. This openness will also extend to your PD meetings.

FROM THE PRINCIPAL'S DESK

Being truly transparent about teaching practices also means making performance and progress public for the whole school. In my school, we post data on our walls and on doors, so nothing is hidden. Every teacher knows where everyone else is. And at every interim assessment there's a data day, where we share data with each other around state assessments, classroom assessments, attendance, behavior, and discipline. (You'll read more about this in Chapter Six.) Often these days are times of celebration as we encourage each other's success.

Transparency and accountability are huge issues in improving school performance. It's about holding people accountable. In most underperforming schools, you will not see people being held accountable for their data. You won't see that data posted in the school. Some administrators want to protect their teachers from the data, but school improvement is not about protecting people. It's about taking ownership of what isn't working and doing something about it.

As important as this transparency is, you'll sometimes need to make some accommodations to best help your teachers grow and improve. I once met with a teacher whom I'd been coaching. The preconference wasn't going very well. She was getting a lot of unsatisfactories from me, and I could see her deflating. At that moment, the chief of my school network walked in. (In Chicago, schools in close proximity are grouped in networks to promote collaboration and sharing.) The chief is a hands-on person and wanted to join our conversation. But I noticed that the teacher immediately became very uncomfortable.

I took the chief aside briefly and explained the situation. She understood, said she would meet with me later, and left. The teacher thanked me profusely and said she wouldn't have been able to answer any more questions with my chief present.

The teacher went on to tell me that she didn't quite understand the questions. That's why she hadn't been putting down the right information. I thanked her for being honest and said, "I don't want to send you into the classroom and have you bomb when I observe you. As your instructional leader, my role is to set you up for success. I definitely don't want to embarrass you in front of our boss. I'm glad my chief left the room while we wrapped up."

You may encounter similar situations in your school. The most important thing is that you make your staff feel comfortable when their teaching practices are being questioned. It's important that teachers understand that they're safe when they're vulnerable and that you're on their side. Instructional leadership is not about catching teachers at their worst and throwing their weaknesses at them. Instead, it's about helping teachers become solid practitioners when they're in front of students. When teachers feel they can trust you, you'll be able to have the necessary conversations with them.

#8: INSTILL A SENSE OF OWNERSHIP AMONG TEACHERS

Teachers need to own and accept that what happens in their classrooms is a direct result of what they do or don't do. Classroom problems don't "just happen." Some teachers don't want to take that responsibility. Instead, they blame students, parents, or the community: "I taught it and they just didn't get it." With your leadership—and your modeling of taking responsibility when you need to do so yourself—you'll build a staff that will say: "I taught it, but something I did resulted in not everyone getting it." And, with the help of PD, they'll make adjustments and do a better job of teaching the material the next time.

This can take time. I once had a conversation with a new teacher who was having trouble managing her class. I asked her to reflect on why her students didn't respect her. What message was she sending so that students felt they could misbehave in front of her without consequences? I told her, "That's something you have to own, because I'm not in that classroom all day. I can come in and get things in order, but I can't stay there. Building respect and relationships with students is something you've got to do."

She resisted taking ownership. Her response was, "That's just the way the students are." And to some degree that's true. Students don't always do what we ask them to do. In addition, some parents use discipline methods at home that we don't use in school, and that can make our jobs more challenging when it comes to classroom management. Nevertheless, the teacher is responsible for her students during the school day, and she must work with each student and his behavior issues where they are.

In my experience, when teachers fail to take ownership, it's usually around classroom management issues. In contrast, it's very rare for someone to disown his data. Teachers are usually pretty good at accepting what the data says about their classroom practices, and after assessments that show areas of concern, teachers typically recognize that they need help in making sure their students succeed. This allows you, as the administrative leader, to make the most of PD.

Another way teachers may fail to take ownership is by not feeling connected to the entire student body. For example, tension sometimes arises between general education teachers and special education teachers who teach diverse learners and students with special needs.

As a visionary leader, you can work to foster the attitude that everyone is in this together, no matter what types of students they teach or what successes or setbacks you might encounter. These are conversations that you can have on an ongoing basis.

One system I've used that may also help you is empowering teachers to give out small amounts of school money to any student—not just those in their own classes—which students can then spend in the school store. For instance, if a teacher is walking down the hallway and sees a class behaving well, he can say to them, "I really like the way you have shown maturity in the hallway going to the restroom. I'm going to give coins for the school store to each one of you." This practice encourages teachers to praise behavior beyond their own classes, and it also helps students feel valued by the entire staff.

Also encourage teachers to visit and learn from other classrooms on a regular basis. Consider establishing peer observations, in which teachers can observe their colleagues with a specific focus in mind. You can set up these observations for teachers who need help, but also for your Instructional Leadership Team. It helps for your ILT to regularly observe classrooms so that when you discuss problems in practice, they have a sense of what you've been observing and have some perspective to bring to the table. In addition to observing and coaching teachers who have a weakness in a certain area, ILT members will also conduct general observations to get a feel for where the teachers are as a whole. They're not necessarily looking for problems. In some cases they may be observing a teacher who's particularly good at a specific lesson or standard. These observations can then inform your practice of PD.

#9: USE VETERAN TEACHERS TO SUPPORT NEW TEACHERS

It's important that you have a plan to make new teachers feel welcome, prepared, and supported, because they may come to you not knowing exactly how to get started in the classroom. Use veteran teachers to help support these novice teachers and make them feel valued. Veterans can lead PD for newer teachers, which might take place either in the classroom or in PD meetings. You can also pair up new teachers with experienced teachers as grade-level partners. The veteran teachers will be able to answer questions that you or another staff member may not be around to answer. As the administrator, you won't be able to get into everyone's classroom every day, but a veteran teacher can work with a new teacher to achieve your goals. A sub can cover one of the rooms so that the experienced teacher can go into the new teacher's room to observe, or vice versa. For example, near the beginning of one school year, I had a seasoned teacher lead a professional development session on a specific classroom management strategy. Several new teachers were impressed and later set up times to visit her room to observe her practice.

By drawing on the experience of your veteran teachers in this way, you begin to build a professional learning community where everyone is recognized and learns from each other.

#10: USE TECHNOLOGY TO HELP BOOST STUDENT ACHIEVEMENT

Many schools, particularly in low-income areas, don't have high-tech teaching aids, and principals may not be inclined to get them, feeling that limited funds are better spent elsewhere. However, technology has an important role to play throughout elementary and middle school. Today's students are very comfortable with technology, and you can capitalize on that to enhance instruction and boost achievement. By the time students get to high school and college, technology will only be more advanced. If you don't have it in your school, your students will be at a disadvantage.

Of course, that doesn't mean you need to acquire every brand-new gadget. Depending on your budget and the needs of your students, you can consider a number of different tools. For instance, interactive whiteboards have large screens and a range of applications around different subject areas, mainly math and science. Lessons can be found on different education websites. Other tools include high-tech overhead projectors; devices that make regular whiteboards interactive; and netbooks and other relatively inexpensive laptops.

You may need to get creative with your school's spending in order to obtain the technology you believe you need. If you're confident that technology could help raise your scores and get your students more engaged in teaching and learning, you might have to prioritize these high-tech tools over other budget items.

Similarly, if your access to technology is limited due to funding issues, try spreading around what you've got. If resources are limited, you might be able to start out with tablets for students a grade level at a time, for instance. Or, if you have only one room full of desktop computers, schedule a class there for every student, even if it's only once a week. Or, if you've created a netbook lab, you might be able to use educational support personnel rather than a tenured teacher in the room. That will save some money and potentially allow you to purchase more.

Also think about funding sources beyond your own budget. Look for potential donors among neighborhood businesses. Apply for grants to pay for technology. Conduct research on contests for schools to win technology tools. The important thing is to do whatever you can to provide your classrooms with what they need for everyone to be successful.

EXPECT TEACHER RESISTANCE TO TECHNOLOGY

You may find, as I have, that some of your staff are hesitant to embrace new technology—especially older teachers. They may worry that they'll struggle to learn how to use new tools, or they may simply feel that their old methods are just fine. If you do encounter this situation, be persistent in pushing teachers to get comfortable with newer tools. Tell teachers, "I want to see technology support in your lesson plan. How are you going to use it in your lessons next week?" You can also offer to set up training sessions to help bring everyone up to speed.

On the flip side, you may also have teachers who love high-tech tools a bit *too* much. I have had teachers who would keep their students in front of computers all day long if they could. Technology is a tool to get some of the results that you're looking for, but it's only one tool. Teachers still need to teach. They need to give some direct instruction. Discussion must take place in the classroom, and students need to interact and work together. When students spend too much time in front of computer screens, they miss out on a vital part of their education.

When you're introducing new technology at your school, start with those teachers who are most enthusiastic about it and can ignite some enthusiasm among their more reluctant colleagues. Once you have a few teachers who can take your vision and move forward with it, you can let them take the lead among their colleagues in using technology. As an administrator, you've got plenty of other things coming your way.

#11: MAKE TIME FOR CELEBRATION AND ENCOURAGEMENT

You might be surprised at how much it can boost morale when you acknowledge something noteworthy or beneficial to your staff. Do this throughout the year. I think it's especially important to celebrate after assessments. A lot of schools simply present the data to their teachers. It can look very foreign and be difficult to decipher.

When assessment data comes back, you can share gains and "quick wins" with the staff. You could bring in balloons and cupcakes, or hand out certificates for specific accomplishments. Most importantly, give encouragement all around—find something in everyone's data to celebrate. It's key to send the message that you're not going to beat yourselves up over what the data looks like, but will instead find things to celebrate. When I was principal at Curtis School of Excellence, it had once been one of the lowest scoring schools in Chicago. The school still had a ways to go, but it was a far cry from where it began. So I celebrated every little step we took toward our goals.

These celebrations don't have to be major. You might give a paper star or some other kudos to Ms. Estepa for a lesson you observed. You could provide teachers with fresh flowers one week to brighten their desks and classrooms. You can also report celebrations in your staff bulletin so everyone stays in the loop about the progress your school is making and the hard work everyone is doing.

Structuring Professional Development at Your School

Building PD into your school usually involves issues of time, scheduling, and teacher compensation. When you hire new staff, I recommend requiring teachers to sign a document saying they are willing to participate in professional development outside of school hours, and specifying—if possible—that teachers will be paid for that extra time. Aim to spend two hours in PD every week engaged in conversations about the structure of the classrooms, the curriculum, and all other components of the school organization.

If your budget doesn't accommodate paying teachers extra for PD time, don't abandon your PD plans. Instead, work on other ways to implement this essential practice. I worked at a school one year where we didn't have enough money to pay for PD. We came up with the idea of "banking time" so that teachers could have PD within the school day and would not have to be given extra compensation. Students remained in class 15 minutes longer each day, and we dismissed them early every other Wednesday. This schedule allowed teachers two hours of PD, from 1 p.m. to 3 p.m., every two weeks.

The fact is professional development won't work very well if you only meet once a month or every two months. That's simply not enough time if you're talking about developing your staff, improving your practices, and transforming good teachers into great ones. So find places within the schedule when teachers can come together. Here's an example of several kinds of PD meetings you could implement in a combination that works for you:

- Every Wednesday, bring in subs to cover for the teachers. Hold full-group data dialogues to assess your progress and talk about ongoing strategies for improvement.
- Assign each teacher and his or her grade-level partner the same prep period. When their kids go to specialty classes, such as PE or music, they're free to do planning and talk about lessons.
- Every other Tuesday, have all clusters (primary, middle, and upper) meet. (Sometimes this requires subs to cover a couple of classes.) It's a good practice to have all cluster teachers come together once in a while, so they can talk about their various classrooms and share the best ways to support their students' transition to the next grade.
- Choose one day each week or every other week to devote teachers' prep periods to principal-directed PD.

In many schools, but particularly those that are struggling or under-performing, PD tends to be more intensive during the summer and early in the school year. Teachers do not have to give up their summers to do professional development, but I do recommend trying to lock in at least three consecutive days of PD training before school starts, or four days within a two-week period after school begins, for a really powerful start to the school year. During this time, you'll talk about areas that are working well, along with areas for growth. That way, your entire staff will be starting the year on the same page, because everybody will have been in PD together and gotten the same message.

Find places within the schedule when teachers can come together.

Conducting a Professional Development Meeting

When I was a classroom teacher, my experience with professional development wasn't great. We didn't get the opportunity to collaborate with colleagues, ask questions, clarify our thinking, and summarize what we'd learned. Instead, PD had a top-down structure with the principal saying, "I want you to do this." That was it. Meetings were perfunctory and rote, and my fellow teachers and I usually left them feeling dispirited, because there was no buy-in or accountability. We went back to our classrooms and did whatever we wanted in isolation. We knew no one was going to follow up with us.

From that experience, I've learned how to make PD meetings relevant and engaging. Here are tips on how to lead your meetings.

- Share group norms at the start of each meeting, with an emphasis on how to give and hear constructive criticism in an effective way.
- Talk about specific goals you want teachers to leave with that day. Hand out an agenda, listing the topics you will cover in PD. (For an example of PD meeting agendas, see Figure 8 on page 118.)
- Rotate leadership among various staff members. Leaders could include you, a dean, an experienced teacher, or a new teacher. It's powerful when you tap into more than one person to offer professional leadership and advice. It can be especially valuable for a new teacher to have this leadership role.
- Always allow time for collaboration, sharing, and questions. Give the teachers sufficient time to work together. Ask teachers to give feedback on the presentation. Ask them to summarize professional literature or compare ideas. They might share something they saw or did at another school, or may offer a new perspective. We were discussing team teaching at one meeting, which prompted two teachers to share their previous team teaching experiences. Check in with teachers throughout the meeting: How did that feel for you? How did you connect with that? Allow everyone to ask questions and clarify their thinking.
- Be prepared to give up some authority. Allow teachers to bounce ideas off each other without intervening or commenting. You often won't know what your colleagues are going to say. They may not say what

FIGURE 8: **TWO SAMPLE PROFESSIONAL DEVELOPMENT AGENDAS**

PD Meeting Agenda 1: Setting the Tone for Excellence (Content)	PD Meeting Agenda 2: Creating a Data-Craving Culture
• Teacher Orientation and Restructured Vote • Balanced Literacy Overview • Word Their Way Overview (facilitated by Ms. Carson) • ANET Overview (facilitated by Mr. Cahill) • Conceptual Math (facilitated by Ms. Schmidt) • Science Overview (facilitated by Mr. Letterman) • Goals for Professional Learning Communities • Reflection and Announcements	• Data Talks; Data Walks; Data Cluster Meetings • Guided Reading and Daily 5 (facilitated by Mr. Jones) • Guided Math (facilitated by Ms. Foster) • One-on-One Goal Setting Progress Checks (using Danielson) • Reflection and Announcements

you're thinking or say it another way. But allowing this openness is a powerful way to exchange new kinds of experiences and ideas.

• Summarize the big ideas at the end of each meeting. In my school we end our PD time with a reflection tool, where participants write down their thoughts or "takeaways" from the session. You can also use Exit Tickets to gauge what teachers are getting out of the meetings. Ask them to answer a couple of questions about what was most useful to them or what suggestions and questions they might have. They don't have to put their names on their responses. Discuss the answers with your Instructional Leadership Team to decide on follow-up steps. This feedback will help you answer questions at future meetings. You could share common questions or concerns in the staff bulletin, memo, email, or devote another PD meeting to a particular topic that was raised.

Outside your meetings, continue to check in with teachers in the same way they check in with their students. When you meet one-on-one, continue to keep PD in mind. Ask questions to encourage them to think about and reflect on their practice and how to improve it. By encouraging reflection, you'll get information that will help you determine whether you should be visiting a teacher's classroom for another week or two, or can move on to a new observation.

When you implement these kinds of practices, the focus of your professional development meetings will shift to student learning, and your instructional practices will begin to change. Regular and intentional conversations around instruction not only promote a deeper understanding of teaching and learning but also build a greater sense of trust and camaraderie among your staff. That powerful combination will help you transform your school and achieve your goals.

Room for Reflection

PROFESSIONAL DEVELOPMENT

- Have your views of professional development changed after reading this chapter?

- What changes in professional development do you plan to make after reading this chapter?

- List three goals for improving professional development during the coming school year or term. How will you achieve them?

- How will you differentiate or tailor professional development for veteran teachers and novice teachers?

- What data points will you use to develop PD for your staff?

LESSON PLAN FEEDBACK FORM

Teacher _____

Observer _____

Date _____

LESSON COMPONENT	EVIDENT	COMMENT
Learning Goal/Specific Skill	☐ Yes ☐ No	
Modeling *(I Do)*	☐ Yes ☐ No	
Guided Practice *(We Do)*	☐ Yes ☐ No	
Independent Practice *(You Do)*	☐ Yes ☐ No	
Small Groups	☐ Yes ☐ No	
Homework	☐ Yes ☐ No	
Other	☐ Yes ☐ No	

CHAPTER SIX
The Specifics of Instructional Leadership

At the end of the school year, your superiors will want to know a few key things: Did you move the numbers? Did a certain number of students grow to a certain percentile in academic achievement? Did students demonstrate academic excellence in the classroom and on standardized tests? For better or worse, that's your mandate as a school administrator. To transform teaching and learning in your school, you need to be an instructional leader— not only in PD meetings, but in each and every classroom.

Many principals struggle to fulfill this role. As a classroom teacher, I rarely saw my principals. Too many spent most of their days in the main office. And there are good reasons to spend some time in your office. Your day-to-day administrative duties may include budgeting, facilities maintenance, scheduling, and dealing with schoolwide discipline. These are important duties in any school. However, if student achievement is to rise, administrators must be deeply involved in curriculum and instructional delivery. This means getting out of the main office and taking a hands-on, interactive approach to monitoring, coaching, and improving classroom instruction.

The idea of spending most of the day out of your office may be a change for you, but it's essential that you learn to master it. The exact way you break down your day will depend on your school's needs, strengths, and goals. As an example, here's what I do: I spend at least 40 percent of my day observing teachers in classrooms and another 30 percent in instructional feedback and coaching. The remaining 30 percent is spent on day-to-day operations and parent or community relations. So a full 70 percent of my day is spent on instructional leadership. Again, this may sound like a lot if you're not used to it. But I have seen firsthand how powerful it is when a principal plays this role. If you aren't being an instructional leader, you're just being a manager, and that role doesn't work for principals who are working to change their schools.

In addition, aim for every teacher on your staff to have a one-on-one coaching relationship with you or with another staff member. Stay up to date with what each teacher is working on through coaching.

An instructional leader transforms the way teachers think. When principals are observing classroom instruction on a daily basis, the entire school organization understands that teaching and learning are top priorities. This starts with hiring teachers who understand your vision or changing the minds of the people who are already on staff, but that's only the beginning. Training, coaching, and nurturing your staff throughout the school year are all essential to lifting student achievement.

> *An instructional leader transforms the way teachers think.*

Some teachers are unprepared for classrooms where students have varying skill sets and ability levels. They may not know how to handle third-grade classes where some kids are struggling to read and others are reading at a sixth-grade level. If you don't prepare your teachers for that kind of experience—and if you don't convince them that all kids can learn at their pace and that there are specific ways teachers can make that happen—they will not be as effective as they could be in the classroom, and you'll have trouble improving your numbers.

The main difference between effective and ineffective teachers lies in their expectations and attitudes. Effective teachers focus on what they *can* do; ineffective teachers focus on what they can't do. The effective teacher is going to be coachable and open to different ideas, practices, and ways of getting content to students, while an ineffective teacher is more likely to use a "one-size-fits-all" model that doesn't work for every learner.

To improve any school in a meaningful and lasting way, you have to change teachers' minds about expectations and attitudes. You have to constantly coach them about valuable strategies that work in the classroom. You can't focus only on the obvious and visible facets, such as having beautiful, organized classrooms, students sitting in an orderly fashion, and the right postings on the walls. These things aren't unimportant. But real transformation of teaching and learning has to take place from the inside out.

As the instructional leader, you're not just coaching teachers in specific areas of practice, you're setting a broader agenda as well. You must push your staff to be accountable for the teaching and learning that takes place.

This is a good model to use in any school, not just a struggling one. But too often it doesn't happen.

As one example of instructional leadership, you might institute a change in teaching practices by requiring your staff to cluster kids in small groups according to academic readiness. Some teachers may resist this approach. But the fact is that whole-group teaching (sometimes described as "teaching down the middle") has gone out the window as the norm. Overall, it simply doesn't yield good results or raise achievement. Of course, teachers will sometimes choose to do some whole-group teaching, but as an instructional leader, you can make sure it's not their approach for the entire day.

Another example of instructional leadership: Ask every teacher to meet with his grade-level partner and report back to you about what each child should know and be able to do by the end of each grade. What should second graders know and be able to do in preparation for third grade? What should every third grader know going into fourth grade?

Compiling this information requires a lot of cluster time within the grade levels and a lot of vertical planning. But it also challenges teachers to really examine and understand what their students need to know. Not many educators are being pushed in that way. State standards can sometimes be so broad that you need to dissect and break them down so you and your teachers understand exactly what they need to teach. An instructional leader makes sure that when students are ready to take standardized tests, they've been taught everything they need to know in order to be successful on the assessments. By setting specific goals for each grade, you hold yourselves—and each other—accountable. Everyone knows that by the end of second grade all students must be beginning readers; by the end of third grade all students must be comprehensive, fluid readers. Being clear and decisive about your teaching goals helps everyone stay focused on the path to improvement.

In addition to sharing these grade-level goals internally, it's important to share them with parents, as well. That way, each parent is able to approach you or one of your teachers and say, "My child is supposed to know how to put things in sequence. How come she doesn't know how to do that?" Again, this holds you and your staff accountable. If a child hasn't reached his learning goals, someone in the school must be ready and willing to own that shortcoming, and, more importantly, take steps to address the problem.

As you embrace your role as an instructional leader, help your teachers ask and answer these fundamental questions:

- What do my students need to know and how will I teach that information?
- How can I work smarter?
- How can I work more collaboratively with my colleagues and learn from their experience?

Forming an Instructional Leadership Team (ILT)

One of your first tasks as your school's instructional leader is to form an Instructional Leadership Team (ILT). This team is crucial in lifting student achievement and should be organized before or at the very start of the school year. Your ILT will go into classrooms and help coach teachers, which is a core strategy in improving student performance. Forming this in-house team to make coaching a priority means you won't have to pay someone to come in to do professional development, which is often the case in schools without an ILT.

When you assemble your ILT, look for individuals who have expertise in literacy and math, who can lead others, and who can put aside longtime staff relationships to step into a role that's more constructively critical of the instructional process. Work to identify these individuals during your one-on-one staff interviews at the start of the school year (see Chapter Two).

Ideally, the team should consist of the principal, the assistant principal, and at least one other core person. The people assisting you might be "freed staff" who are not connected to specific classrooms, but I also recommend recruiting classroom teachers who are content experts, especially in math and literacy. If your ILT does include classroom teachers, you will need to occasionally free them from their classrooms, for conducting walkthroughs and setting up coaching sessions. However, most ILT meetings can be held after school.

As principal or administrator, you'll need to spend a certain amount of your time on typical organizational issues—budget matters, the custodial staff, an irate parent. You can't always free yourself to be in a classroom at a specific time. The ILT can step in to observe and coach when you can't, and can meet with you weekly to discuss issues, progress, and details such as the instructional focus for the upcoming week. With such a team, you can also provide observation, coaching, and feedback to the entire staff within three days of the start of the year, which you'd be unable to accomplish alone.

The ILT is also necessary to ensure that you're not the only person coming up with ideas. A principal or administrator needs "thought partners," so to speak—people who have expertise in their fields, as well as influence within the school and connections with many people within your organization.

After observing teachers in the classroom and determining who needs coaching, meet with your ILT to discuss what you've seen and what your next steps will be. What feedback has been given to teachers? What has been the reaction? When you return to that classroom, what are you now looking for?

Give each teacher time to make adjustments in his teaching, based on the feedback you've offered. Revisit that classroom the following week to determine if the problem has been addressed. If it hasn't, suggest another way to solve it. If the issue has been managed, move on to observing other aspects of the teacher's performance. Continue this process every week throughout the school year, with every teacher you've identified as needing coaching.

Evaluating an Existing Staff

Your district or state may have guidelines and requirements for teacher evaluations, and if so, you'll need to work within that framework as you develop your school's approach to evaluation. However, you will probably also have some flexibility to create your own methods. I recommend using a system based on Charlotte Danielson's work. Danielson's *Enhancing Professional Practice: A Framework for Teaching* describes four domains: Domain 1: Planning and Preparation; Domain 2: The Classroom Environment; Domain 3: Instruction; and Domain 4: Professional Responsibilities. You can use these domains to frame standards for teacher excellence and grade teacher evaluations according to these standards.

I also advise splitting your teacher evaluations into two observations: A formal one and an informal one. In Chicago, our formal observation is very structured, and it's mandatory that the administrator conduct it. Whatever your school or district requires, I have found that it's extremely useful to have the teacher complete preconference questions ahead of the formal observation, which will give you a snapshot of what you'll talk about. Then you can sit down with the teacher for a preconference meeting to discuss the lesson you'll be observing. Ask the teacher to walk you through everything that's going to happen. Finally, set a date and time for your visit to her classroom.

When you do visit the teacher's classroom for the formal observation, take a laptop, tablet, or notebook so you can take detailed notes about everything that happens in the room during that period. Tag everything that happens with one of the four Danielson domains. Domain 1, about lesson planning, can be evaluated before you conduct the observation. Domains 2 and 3 are pretty much what you will see during your time in the classroom. Domain 4, professional responsibilities, is not about classroom observation but is based on questions teachers answer about various aspects of their practice, such as communicating with parents about grades and attendance, submitting grades on time, and so on.

Each domain has different components, and you can tag things based on both the domain and the specific component. This information can go into your school's database, with the teacher's performance on each component scored as Unsatisfactory, Basic, Proficient, or Distinguished. Teachers who score in the Basic and Unsatisfactory categories will be placed on a remediation or PD plan. A teacher could also lose her job if she doesn't improve her practices.

The next step is to meet again with the teacher for a post-conference discussion about how you scored her observation. Encourage the teacher to talk about things she has reflected on in the time since your observation—techniques she would have changed or moments that jumped out at her during the observation. These reflections can be added to your notes as well.

Depending on what you observe, some teachers will receive two informal and formal evaluations. Other teachers will receive just one of each.

The informal part of the observation takes place when you or members of your ILT visit classrooms unannounced. These informal observations will probably last only about twenty minutes and will evaluate the teacher for Domains 2 and 3 only.

Time management will be a critical part of your evaluation planning. The entire evaluation process can take five or six hours per teacher. You'll have to review all of your notes, record them using software or some other system, and share that with the teacher before your post-conference meeting so that she gets to see everything you've noted as the evaluator. You'll then meet to discuss your findings. Conduct this evaluation annually with your entire staff, not just new hires.

Danielson's four domains can be a great tool for coaching teachers throughout the year, in addition to carrying out evaluations. For example, if a teacher needs to strengthen certain instructional skills, she and her coach could start by focusing on Domain 3b, which is about using questioning and discussion techniques.

On pages 141–143 is a coaching tool focused on evaluating Danielson's Domains 2 and 3. You could use this or a similar model to evaluate your staff. On pages 144–145 is another evaluation tool that uses Danielson's Domains 2 and 3 (as well as general classroom observation) to assess teachers' performance and determine where they need additional support.

You can use the subsets of each Danielson domain to initiate professional development conversations with teachers: "The last time I was in your classroom, I observed that there weren't enough questions being asked or the right kinds of questions. I would like to coach you on this for the next five or six weeks." Instead of tackling all of Domain 3, you can pinpoint areas that you want teachers to work on. If you have a new teacher, you may want to focus on Domain 2, which is classroom environment. Maybe you want this teacher to work on managing student behavior and establishing the right norms and expectations in the classroom. For example, you could look at Domain 2d (managing student behavior) for the next five or six weeks. The more focused your evaluations are, the more your teachers will improve in their classroom practices.

The Specifics of Classroom Observation

I recommend conducting three kinds of classroom observation:

1. **Formal observations:** A formal observation usually lasts forty-five to sixty minutes, and it's planned ahead of time. You will have already discussed with teachers the date, time, and lesson plan. Take detailed notes at these observations.
2. **Informal observations:** This type of observation usually lasts no longer than fifteen minutes, and it is not scheduled with the teacher ahead of time. Take brief notes.
3. **Check-in visits:** Like informal observations, these visits will be brief and usually unannounced. They may last as little as five to ten minutes. When I do these visits, I may or may not take detailed notes,

but I do usually use "Wows and Wonders" (see page 109 for more information) or make note of "quick wins" I can share with teachers.

On a day that you conduct classroom observations, begin your day with your normal routine, such as saying good morning to students as they enter the school. Then visit each classroom and say good morning to teachers and students. Spend some time popping in and out of classrooms—not conducting observations, but just getting a feel for things.

When you do get started with your observations, look for a variety of things: classroom environment, management, specific instructional areas, objectives, activities, and pacing. Again, be sure teachers understand that you're not trying to catch them making mistakes. Rather, make it clear that you're being supportive in helping them grow as professionals in improving their craft.

You may want to visit some classrooms twice a day, in the morning and afternoon, to compare those two time periods. This can be especially helpful with new teachers, since mornings tend to be a bit better organized and managed for inexperienced teachers than the afternoons. Also consider visiting classrooms twice a day in September. After the summer vacation, mornings generally go well, but by noon everyone is tired. No one has yet built up the stamina to work until the final bell without some kind of release or relaxation. Once the year progresses, afternoons will become just as tight as the mornings for most teachers. You may need to continue visiting some classrooms twice a day, however.

Again, during informal observations, you don't need to stay longer than fifteen or twenty minutes. Similarly, it's not always necessary to take notes. Walk around the classroom to get a feel for everyone's energy level.

When you do check-ins, you may want to carry "Wow" and "Wonder" cards (see page 109 for more information) and use these to comment on what you see. For example, "Wow, there was so much engagement happening! You did a great job of keeping students from sliding under the radar by giving them another chance to answer questions," and "I wonder if you could have done more asking for understanding." Then you can leave these cards on the teacher's desk before you leave without having to interrupt instruction.

During all observations, it's important to look for some specific signs of effective classroom management and teaching. The following thirteen tools and techniques are examples of important things to watch for and assess.

#1: THE MARKERBOARD CONFIGURATION

The markerboard configuration is a simple but important classroom tool. It displays the classroom's agenda and goals, including schedule, subject-specific goals, and homework. This should be in a consistent location every day so you don't have to search for it. Make sure the teacher is assigning homework. In some classes teachers assign homework packets on Monday and they're not due until Friday. In other classes homework is assigned daily. There should never be a day when you walk up to a student and say, "What's your homework?" or "Did you do your homework?" and he replies, "I didn't have any." Of course, in any classroom, you may hear from a student that she didn't do her homework. But that shouldn't be because the teacher didn't assign it.

Figure 9 on page 130 is an example of a well-organized markerboard configuration. Objectives should be clear, measurable, and manageable.

#2: DO NOWS AND EXIT TICKETS

Do Nows and Exit Tickets are two simple but powerful mini-assessments given by the classroom teacher. Do Nows happen before a lesson begins. An example might be a third-grade teacher listing three words that will be key to a lesson and asking students to define them.

Exit Tickets assess what students have learned at the end of a lesson. The teacher might ask students to circle three words in a story and list their antonyms or synonyms. Or the teacher might take a relevant question from an upcoming assessment, change it in some way, and ask students to answer it.

According to what time you walk into a classroom, you might not see either of these assessments. The teacher might be in the middle of a mini-lesson or some guided practice. The Do Now has already been done, and the Exit Tickets haven't been given out yet. Still, keep an eye out for samples of these two items, and make sure they're reflected in the lesson plans. I like to collect an extra copy or sample of a mini-assessment while I'm in the classroom. Later I may use these samples as starting points for discussion with teachers and the ILT. For instance, questions to ask about a Do Now might include:

- How is this assessment aligned to the standards?
- Does it build on students' background knowledge?
- Is it rigorous enough for the grade level?

FIGURE 9: SAMPLE FOURTH-GRADE MARKERBOARD CONFIGURATION

AGENDA/SCHEDULE	OBJECTIVES
8:15–8:30 Do Now/Breakfast **8:30–9:00** Writing **9:00–10:00** Math **10:00–10:10** Restroom **10:10–11:10** Prep/Library **11:15–12:00** Lunch/Recess **12:00–1:15** Literacy **1:15–1:25** Restroom **1:25–2:15** Social Studies **2:15–3:10** Science **3:15** Dismissal	*Students will be able to...* **Math** • Use models, manipulatives, and arrays to represent multiplication with 85 percent mastery. (For example: *The array to the right represents 3 x 2 or 2 x 3.*) • Identify the factor and product in a multiplication sentence with 85 percent mastery. (For example: *In 3 x 2 = 6, 3 and 2 are the factors, 6 is the product.*) **Social Studies** • Identify the steps by which a bill becomes federal law in the United States. **Literacy/Writing** • Read and make inferences based on Chapter Five of text *Roll of Thunder, Hear My Cry.* • Write a short story from Cassie's point of view. **Science** • Use sequencing skills to construct a miniature kite. **Homework** • Students will make arrays out of household items (such as beans or pennies). • Complete math assignment on page 14. • Read Chapter Six of *Roll of Thunder, Hear My Cry*

#3: CONTENT KNOWLEDGE

Does the teacher know what he's talking about? Does he have strong knowledge of the standards and effective ways to move students to mastery? Listen to the teacher's delivery of the instruction. Is it in effective, kid-friendly language, or is the teacher speaking above students' heads?

#4: PACING AND URGENCY

Is the instructional time being maximized? Is the teacher spending too much time in teacher talk and going on and on? Or is she quickly moving from each part of her agenda or lesson to the next to maximize the time and cover more of the content? Does the lesson have a sense of purpose and intent?

Beginning teachers often get stuck in their lessons. Because they want to make sure that students understand, they tend to overexplain. While some students may need the constant explanation and repetition, teachers lose time when they get stuck there.

#5: MODELING AND MINI-LESSONS (I DO)

In explaining the lesson, is the teacher modeling, step-by-step, what he expects students to do? Is he demonstrating thinking aloud? Is he modeling the kinds of questions he wants students to ask themselves? All of this is what we call the "I do" part of instruction.

#6: GUIDED PRACTICE (WE DO)

Does the teacher model an activity or lesson for the students, and then lead them through guided practice by saying, "Let's do it together"? Guided practice is extremely important because it provides students with another opportunity to be successful before being released to independent practice. Students are given the chance to practice with the teacher and time to ask questions. During guided practice, teachers should check for understanding and begin gathering information for those students who may require more explicit individual instruction.

#7: INDEPENDENT PRACTICE (YOU DO)

Independent practice asks students to spend a sustained amount of time practicing or doing an assignment the teacher has just given them. I really like independent practice in reading, which is important preparation for state tests. If teachers haven't built independent reading practice into their day, some students may get lost in the second sentence of a four-page essay during assessment. They might skip the reading and jump to the questions and write down anything that comes to mind. Teachers need to set aside time during the day to allow students to read independently, while checking in with them to make sure they understand what they're reading and are not frustrated by it. Once teachers have introduced independent reading practice, teachers can build upon this practice every day. For instance, in second-grade classrooms, students could start out reading independently for five minutes and gradually increase that time to twenty or thirty minutes a day. This helps lay the foundations for third grade, when students will need to be able to read long passages and answer questions.

#8: ACADEMIC RIGOR

Look for rigor. Is there grade-level complexity? Are there rigorous questions and high-level applications and activities? Or is this low-level instruction?

Here's an example. Once, when I walked into an eighth-grade classroom, I saw students cutting out vocabulary words and pasting them into a book. I wouldn't be surprised or bothered to see kids cutting and pasting in a kindergarten class, but in eighth grade it's unacceptable.

In your evaluations, part of your job is to identify this type of inappropriate instruction and point it out to the teacher. Push your teachers to always make their lessons as rigorous as possible. Doing so will move students from the middle rungs to the highest rungs of achievement.

#9: DIFFERENTIATED INSTRUCTION

Look for differentiated instruction. Every classroom will have students of different ability levels. In a third-grade classroom, some students may be functioning at a first-grade level in some areas, while others might be at fifth-grade levels. Given this reality, what is the teacher doing to meet the needs of all students?

Differentiation is a powerful strategy to address this situation. It's about more than varied ability levels. It also addresses learning modalities, learning differences, and unique special needs. Differentiation helps teachers tailor content, process, and product to their students' strengths and weaknesses.

If teachers are new to differentiation, ask them to start by focusing on varied ability levels. If you simply ask teachers to differentiate their lessons, some may not know where to begin. But if you ask them to think about varied ability levels in their classrooms, that should get them thinking along the right lines. They can start by looking at data to figure out which students are working below, at, and above grade level. From there, ask them to consider how they can support their students based on their abilities. The instructional tasks, products, and assessments will be different for each student, but, in my administrative experience, not all teachers are ready to tap into different learning modalities right away. If that's the case at your school, then that's a necessary PD conversation.

For *all* students to be successful, teachers need to be flexible and adaptable. They need to make content understandable for a student working at a lower level—*and* challenging enough for a student working at a higher level. This might mean teaching to small groups with similar learning goals or using other strategies.

#10: ANCHOR CHARTS

An anchor chart is a visual presentation of a lesson that students can refer back to for help. If you walk into a classroom and don't see anchor charts on the walls, that's a red flag. For me, the presence of these charts confirms that a teacher has been teaching. The classroom should speak for itself, without the teacher saying a word. You should be able to look around the classroom and say, "I see that they've done a lesson on probability. I see that they've done some fractions or an extended response."

Extended responses are customary on standardized tests. Students are given a reading prompt and have to write an essay. The question may be: "In the story you just read, Alice was surprised at her birthday party. Why was Alice surprised? Discuss the last time you were surprised."

An anchor chart for an extended response could say at the top, "Extended Response, Step One: Restate the prompt," followed by a sample of how students can do that. Another step may be, "Go back to the passage and find something that relates to the prompt."

These step-by-step instructions should be posted on the classroom's walls. A teacher might use chart paper, a whiteboard, or some other way to display the anchor chart, as long as it's clear and visible. Every time the teacher does an extended response with her class, she should refer to that chart. The students can then refer back to it as they do the next lesson. Anchor charts build instruction.

#11: TEACHER TALK

Is the teacher spending much of the period talking? Or is he pushing students to do a lot of the talking? I once heard the expression: "Whoever is doing most of the talking is doing most of the learning." In some class-rooms, teacher talk will take up the majority of a forty-five-minute period. When that happens, some students are likely to start checking out. To max-imize instructional time, teachers need to pay attention to factors including pacing, urgency, and minimizing teacher talk. All of these skills can be strengthened through coaching.

#12: CHECKING FOR UNDERSTANDING

Does the teacher check to see if students understand directions and concepts? As the teacher is talking, does she do some check-ins so her instruction doesn't turn into a lecture? For example, "Give me a thumbs-up if you understand what I just said" or, "James, please explain what I just said." Is she asking questions regularly to make sure students understand, or is she doing a lot of talking and then saying, "Here's the assignment, go for it"?

If a teacher does a lot of talking and doesn't check for understanding, seventeen hands will go up when the assignment is put in front of students, and the teacher will hear, "What am I supposed to be doing again?" If teachers routinely check for understanding, that's much less likely to happen.

#13: CLASSROOM MANAGEMENT

How are teachers managing their students? Do you see discipline in the classroom? What routines and procedures are in place to ensure safety? Without classroom management, the greatest lesson in the world can fail before it even begins.

Beyond the fundamentals of discipline, classroom management also involves the joy factor and student engagement. Are students bored out of their minds? Or is this a fun class with engaged and enthusiastic students? Is the teacher talking to the four kids who sit in the front, or is the teacher meeting the needs of all students? You want every student to be able to say, "I like this teacher and I enjoy coming to this class, because we learn interesting stuff."

The Specifics of Coaching Teachers One-on-One

After your informal observational visits, ask teachers to come to your office during their free period. If you've seen something really glaring that needs to be addressed immediately, you can even have someone cover their class so you can speak to them right way. You can also coach teachers while they're on prep time, after school, or by phone. Coach teachers at times that are consistent with your culture and schedule, making sure to give teachers the PD and feedback they need in order to grow.

In coaching meetings, remind teachers that you probably won't be able to solve every problem in a single conversation—even if a teacher doesn't have many challenges to address. Let them know that you'll set priorities and you're going to focus on one issue at a time, using small steps if necessary, to get each problem where you want it. Only then will you move on to the next concern.

With most teachers, coaching on a particular issue—such as management or pacing—will take three or four meetings, usually over a period of about two weeks. Teachers may ask you to focus on specific skills: "Ms. Robbins, when you come into my classroom, can you take a look at my pacing?" or, "Could you listen to my questioning and give me some feedback on that?"

When you observe a teacher who's great at a particular practice, empower that teacher by asking him or her to lead a professional development session. You might say, "When I was in your classroom, I saw this great lesson on improper fractions, and everyone needs to know this." Make it a point to include these skilled teachers as instructors in your PD meetings.

Also invite the coaches on your Instructional Leadership Team to hold a "walk through" meeting with you one morning a week. This is a time when they can share what they've observed, and you can share what you've seen, too. Find out if you're on the same page. Are some of you seeing things that others are not? Are you moving a weaker teacher to proficiency? Are you moving a proficient teacher to distinguished? If you find that you're not doing that, you need to go back to the table and rethink your coaching strategies.

After a three-month period, conduct a teacher development dialogue with your ILT. Rank your teachers and plan the next stages of coaching. Continue this process every three months.

Prioritizing Your Coaching

As you're observing and coaching teachers, keep in mind your possible plans and priorities for staff, based on the assessment you conducted at the start of the school year as described in Chapter Three:

1. Keep in place
2. Keep and develop
3. Move to another position
4. Observe further
5. Replace (low priority)
6. Replace (high priority)

To a certain extent, all teachers receive the same coaching and PD. However, the teachers you intend to replace—both those you've identified as high priority and low priority—are going to be your primary focus and should receive special attention. That attention has to be given in a careful and intentional way.

For example, the teacher whom I observed cutting and pasting with her eighth-grade class was a high-priority replacement. I initially made the mistake of not being explicit with her about needing more intensive support and coaching and explaining clearly that if she didn't improve she would have to be replaced. As a result, she often felt I was picking on her when I came into her room, when I was actually trying to help her keep her job. In this case, the teacher's walls went up, she fought the coaching, and I eventually did replace her.

Looking back, I realized that I had failed to initiate the difficult conversation I needed to have with her. I should have said, early in the process, "I'm coming into your room to help grow your practice, to lead you in a way that will be beneficial for your teaching and your students. If we can't strengthen your practice, you may be more comfortable teaching somewhere else." With a high-priority teacher, it's important that you are as transparent as possible. Make sure he understands your intent and is open to being coached. Otherwise, the teacher will think you're trying to catch him making mistakes.

In many school districts, administrators must demonstrate that they are supporting a poorly performing teacher. Some teachers can turn it around based on the help you provide. You can design PD to specifically target a teacher's areas of weakness. The teachers who are your top priority for replacement will need the most intensive coaching and PD. You may need to help them understand that observation and coaching might feel a bit uncomfortable. Your core team will be in their classrooms, asking them questions, and pushing them to think and do things differently. But all this attention is designed to help the teacher. So be sure you have the difficult conversations as soon as coaching begins.

Teacher Improvement Plans

A detailed Teacher Improvement Plan (TIP) can help struggling teachers make the most of coaching by clearly outlining the issues they need to fix and how that will be accomplished. It will show these teachers that by working together, you're going to help them improve their practice. For an example of a plan, see Figure 10 on page 138.

The TIP includes a self-reflection component, in which the teacher reflects on what he or she needs to do to improve in the coming weeks. A form to use in this reflection is provided on pages 146–147.

As with all aspects of coaching, it's important to present a Teacher Improvement Plan in the right way. Be clear and direct about what the plan will involve, and emphasize that the plan is designed to help the teacher. You could say to teachers: "Let's sit down and decide what we need to work on. On a regular basis—every day or every other day—you and I will touch base on where we are. I may come into your room every Tuesday and spend forty-five minutes there, looking at the issues we discussed. We'll revisit the plan next month to see if we need to tweak anything. At that point, you may have done really well in one area, and we'll choose to move on to something else."

Another thing to emphasize in coaching and PD situations is that, as you and your staff transform teaching and learning, your vision goes beyond standardized tests. As a team, you're preparing your students to go out into the world, become productive citizens, get quality jobs, and do all the wonderful things you know they can do. You want them to be great thinkers outside the classroom. That's the goal—preparing them for high school, college, and the world beyond. It all starts under your guidance as an instructional leader. You'll never hear me say that we're teaching to a test. Instead, you'll always hear me say, "College begins here."

> *As a team, you're preparing your students to go out into the world.*

FIGURE 10: **SAMPLE TEACHER IMPROVEMENT PLAN**

Teacher: Ms. Smith   **School:** Great School Academy   **Date:** January 5

PURPOSE

At this point in the school year, Ms. Smith consistently demonstrates a strong work ethic and is a team player on the Great School Academy staff. She has clearly established her authority in the classroom and her physical environment is inviting. Based on recent interim assessment data, approximately 50 percent of students in Ms. Smith's classroom are learning third-grade material. It is imperative that Ms. Smith improve her ability to engage all students in learning. She is familiar with the important concepts in the discipline but levels of rigor are not developmentally appropriate. Observed instruction is mostly whole group, with excessive teacher talk. Student literacy assessment (STEP) has not been completed. The purpose of this plan is to address the following targeted areas for improvement in January and February, with a specific focus on the literacy block.

TARGETS FOR IMPROVEMENT (Danielson):

1C: Setting Instructional Outcomes
3E: Engaging Students in Learning
4A: Professional Reflection

1C: Setting Instructional Outcomes	Current Performance: UNSATISFACTORY	Improvement Goal: BASIC
Summary of observations: Observed lessons tend to lack fourth-grade rigor. Word study lessons are stated as activities. In some reading lessons and assignments, the expected outcome is unclear and students do not seem to understand why or how they are to meet the objective. Ms. Smith's math lessons tend to be stronger than literacy. Ms. Smith does not demonstrate a strong background in the literacy continuum.	• Outcomes represent lack of rigor and lack connection to sequence of learning. • Outcomes are not clear or are stated as activities, not as student learning. • Outcomes reflect only one type of learning and only one discipline or strand. • Outcomes are not suitable for the class.	• Outcomes represent moderately high rigor and some connection to sequence of learning. • Outcomes are moderately clear, and at least some are stated as activities. • Outcomes reflect several types of learning, not yet attempting integration of disciplines. • Most outcomes are suitable for most students based on assessments.
3E: Student Engagement	**Current performance: UNSATISFACTORY**	**Improvement Goal: BASIC**
Summary of observations: Ms. Smith's instruction is almost exclusively whole group despite the wide range of student abilities in her class. Sometimes, students participate in the call-and-response activities but appear not to be mentally engaged. Participation through raised hands tends to be limited to a few students. Ms. Smith is high energy and students seem willing to participate with the class, but not necessarily engaged with the lesson content. Ms. Smith's lessons are characterized by excessive teacher talk rather than student talk.	• Activities and assignments are developmentally inappropriate. Students are not mentally engaged. • Instruction groups are inappropriate to the students or instructional outcomes. • Instructional materials and resources are unsuitable to the instructional purposes or do not engage students mentally. • The lesson has no clearly defined structure, or the pace of the lesson is too slow or rushed, or both.	• Activities and assignments are appropriate to some students and engage them mentally, even if others are not yet engaged. • Instructional groups are partially appropriate to the students or moderately successful in advancing the instructional outcomes. • Instructional materials and resources are partially suitable to instructional purposes, or students are partially mentally engaged. • The lesson has a recognizable structure, although it may not yet be uniformly maintained throughout and pacing may be inconsistent.

Sample Teacher Improvement Plan continued

4A: Reflection on Teaching	Current Performance: BASIC	Improvement Goal: PROFICIENT
Summary of observations: Ms. Smith sometimes appears too busy or overwhelmed by responsibilities to participate in reflective conversations and does not generally seek out feedback or coaching, which has occasionally been perceived as a resistance to changing her instructional practice. However, she has expressed an interest in receiving more feedback as a part of the TIP process. She has reached out for support in administering the STEP assessment and is quick to take notes and will make attempts to incorporate new elements of content when requested. She has improved responsiveness to email communication as well.	• Teacher has a generally accurate impression of a lesson's effectiveness and the extent to which instructional outcomes are met. • Teacher makes general suggestions about how a lesson could be improved another time the lesson is taught.	• Teacher makes an accurate assessment of a lesson's effectiveness and the extent to which it achieved its instructional outcomes and can cite general references to support the judgment. • Teacher makes a few specific suggestions of what could be tried another time the lesson is taught.

Frequent observations and feedback from support team.	Weekly; may be unscheduled
Ms. Benjamin will arrange with Ms. Smith to provide weekly support, modeling, and coaching during literacy block to complete assessments (STEP), create instructional groups, curb excessive teacher talk, use lapboards effectively. (Danielson Targets 1C, 3E)	Weekly; 11:00 – 12:30
Ms. Smith and Ms. Benjamin will visit Mr. Carson's fourth-grade small-group teaching during the morning literacy block at the Great School Academy and identify action steps to implement in her own classroom. (Danielson Targets 1C, 3E)	Week of January 17
Ms. Smith will video a 20-minute segment of word study and analyze it for student engagement and levels of rigor with Ms. Benjamin. (All targets)	Begin week of January 10
Ms. Smith will select a professional reading—either Fountas and Pinnell's *Guided Reading* or *The Daily Five*—and complete a weekly reflection journal entry. She will email it to the support team, and Ms. Benjamin will respond to extend the learning. (All targets)	Begin week of January 10
Ms. Benjamin will meet weekly with Ms. Smith to monitor progress. Ms. Smith will be prepared to discuss effectiveness of her lessons and suggestions for ways she will continue to improve instruction. (Danielson Target 4A)	Weekly
Ms. Smith will meet with the support team to evaluate progress and update the action plan as needed. (Danielson Target 4A)	Week of January 31

ACTION PLAN
Teacher acknowledgment:
By signing, I acknowledge that I have read this plan and discussed it with my administrators and coach. I understand the expectations for improvement and the actions I must take in the coming weeks to ensure my teaching practice is at the BASIC performance level.

Teacher's signature _____

Principal's signature _____

Date _____

Room for Reflection

INSTRUCTIONAL LEADERSHIP

- Are you an instructional leader already? If so, what will you do differently after reading this chapter? If not, what steps will you take to become one?

- What changes in coaching do you plan to make after reading this chapter?

- List three instructional leadership goals for the coming school year or term. How will you achieve them?

- Of the thirteen tools and techniques to watch for in classroom observation, which ones stood out to you the most? Why? What new ideas did they give you for conducting observations in your school?

DANIELSON COACHING TOOL

Teacher _____

Subject and/or grade _____

Evaluator _____

Date _____ Time _____

....

Did you observe any components of Balanced Literacy? ☐ Yes ☐ No

If yes, which component(s)? _____

_____

Was the lesson organized and clearly presented? ☐ Yes ☐ No

Danielson Domain	*Classroom Context*	
Domain Two	**Classroom Environment (proficient practice)**	**What to Look For**
2a. Create an environment of respect and rapport	Classroom interactions between the teacher and students are respectful, reflecting warmth and caring and sensitivity to students' culture and levels of development. Student interactions are respectful.	• Teacher/student interactions • Student/student interactions
2b. Establish a culture for learning	The level of energy, from both students and teacher, is high, creating a culture for learning in which the subject is important and students clearly take pride in their work.	• Energy level • High expectations for students/ pride in work
2c. Managing classroom procedures	Little instructional time is lost because of classroom routines and procedures, transitions, handling of supplies, and performance of non-instructional duties, which occur smoothly. Students contribute to classroom routines.	• Organization • Transitions • Classroom routines and procedures
2d. Managing student behavior	Standards of conduct are clear, with teacher's sensitive monitoring of student behavior and subtle response to misbehavior.	• Teacher alertness • Response to misbehavior • Standards of conduct
2e. Organizing physical space	The classroom is safe, and the physical environment ensures the learning of all students and is conducive to the goals of the lesson. Technology is used skillfully, as appropriate to the lesson.	• Room arrangement • Use of technology

Notes on Domain 2
....

Domain 3	Instruction (proficient practice)	What to Look For
3a. Communicating with students	Expectations for learning, directions, and procedures are clear to students. The teacher's explanation of content is effective and anticipates possible student misconceptions.	• Expectations/purpose for lesson • Directions • Explanations
3b. Using questioning and discussion techniques	The teacher's questions are at a high cognitive level, and the teacher allows sufficient time for students to answer. All students participate in the discussion, with the teacher stepping aside when appropriate.	• Teacher questions • Student responses/discussions • Student engagement
3c. Engaging students in learning	Students are engaged throughout the lesson in learning. The activities, student groupings, and the materials are appropriate to the instructional outcomes. The lesson's structure is coherent, with suitable pace.	• Activities and assignments • Instructional groups • Materials and resources • Structure and pacing
3d. Using assessment in instruction	Assessment is used in instruction, through self-assessment by students, monitoring of progress of learning by teacher and/or student, and high-quality feedback to students. Students are fully aware of the assessments criteria used to evaluate their work.	• Student awareness • Teacher monitors/checks for understanding • Feedback to students
3e. Demonstrating flexibility and responsiveness	The teacher seizes an opportunity to enhance learning, building on a spontaneous event or student interests. The teacher adjusts the lesson when needed.	• Adjustments • Persistence

Notes on Domain 3

Describe the overall level of student interest and participation. _____

_____

_____

_____

_____

Describe the overall quality of interpersonal relations between instructor and students. _____

_____

_____

_____

_____

What was particularly effective about the instruction?

_____
_____
_____
_____
_____
_____
_____

What specific suggestions would you make concerning how instruction could be improved?

_____
_____
_____
_____
_____
_____
_____
_____

Initial Summary Message:

_____
_____
_____
_____
_____
_____

Action Plan:

_____
_____
_____
_____
_____
_____
_____

Follow-Up Meeting Date: _____

TEACHER MONITORING TOOL: INFORMAL OBSERVATION

Teacher _____

Subject and/or grade _____

Observer _____

Date _____ Time _____

Establishing a Culture for Learning (Danielson Domain 2: Classroom Environment)

Did you observe:

Lesson Plan Posted	☐ Yes	☐ No
Unit Pacing Guide Posted	☐ Yes	☐ No
Anchor Charts Posted	☐ Yes	☐ No
Current Graded Student Work Displayed	☐ Yes	☐ No
Classroom Library Organized by Genre and Reading Level	☐ Yes	☐ No
Classroom Is Organized and Free of Clutter	☐ Yes	☐ No
Print-Rich Environment	☐ Yes	☐ No
Classroom Objective Posted	☐ Yes	☐ No
Objective Is Aligned to Lesson Plan and Unit Pacing Map	☐ Yes	☐ No

Notes: _____

_____

_____

_____

Classroom Management (Danielson Domain 2: Classroom Environment)

Did you observe:

Clear Code of Conduct Established	☐ Yes	☐ No
Teacher Utilizes Positive Framing to Reinforce Behavior	☐ Yes	☐ No
Teacher Effectively Addresses Inappropriate Behavior	☐ Yes	☐ No

Notes: _____

_____

_____

_____

Engaging Students in Learning (Danielson Domain 3: Instruction)

Did you observe:

Student-to-Student Discourse	☐ Yes	☐ No
Student Access to Complex Text	☐ Yes	☐ No
Task Complexity (Intellectual Engagement)	☐ Yes	☐ No

Learning Tasks Aligned to CCSS   ☐ Yes ☐ No
Differentiation/Data-Driven Flexible Grouping   ☐ Yes ☐ No
Appropriate Structure and Pacing   ☐ Yes ☐ No
Expectation that Students Complete a Learning
    Task or Product During Instruction   ☐ Yes ☐ No

Notes: _____
_____
_____
_____

General Instructional Strategies
Did you observe:

Modeling	☐ Yes ☐ No	Phonics/Word Study	☐ Yes ☐ No
Guided Practice	☐ Yes ☐ No	Lesson Closure	☐ Yes ☐ No
Independent Practice	☐ Yes ☐ No	Math Talks	☐ Yes ☐ No
Shared Reading	☐ Yes ☐ No	Math Lab	☐ Yes ☐ No
Guided Reading	☐ Yes ☐ No	Science Lab	☐ Yes ☐ No

Notes: _____
_____
_____
_____

Strengths: _____
_____
_____
_____
_____
_____

Quick Wins: _____
_____
_____
_____
_____
_____
_____

SELF-REFLECTION TOOL—WINTER BREAK

As teachers, our job is always complex and fast-paced. Winter break is a good time to decompress and gain some perspective on how we're doing. To that end, please take a few minutes at some point during the break to complete this brief self-reflection based on the elements of Charlotte Danielson's framework.

Your thoughtful responses will help focus our coaching conversations and will not be shared with anyone else.

For each element, circle the number that most closely reflects how you feel about this aspect of teaching, and then answer the questions that follow.

0 = I'm really not sure how I'm doing with this one.
1 = Arrghh! I'm not where I want to be with this element.
2 = Some days I think I've got this down, but on other days it falls apart.
3 = I'm feeling pretty good about this element most days.
4 = I am rocking this element all day, every day!

DOMAIN 1: Planning and Preparation
1a: Demonstrating Knowledge of Content and Pedagogy   0 1 2 3 4
1b: Demonstrating Knowledge of Students   0 1 2 3 4
1c: Setting Instructional Outcomes   0 1 2 3 4
1d: Demonstrating Knowledge of Resources   0 1 2 3 4
1e: Designing Coherent Instruction   0 1 2 3 4
1f: Designing Student Assessments   0 1 2 3 4

DOMAIN 2: Classroom Environment
2a: Creating an Environment of Respect and Rapport   0 1 2 3 4
2b: Establishing a Culture for Learning   0 1 2 3 4
2c: Managing Classroom Procedures   0 1 2 3 4
2d: Managing Student Behavior   0 1 2 3 4
2e: Organizing Physical Space   0 1 2 3 4

DOMAIN 3: Instruction
3a: Communicating with Students   0 1 2 3 4
3b: Using Questioning and Discussion Techniques   0 1 2 3 4
3c: Engaging Students in Learning   0 1 2 3 4
3d: Using Assessment in Instruction   0 1 2 3 4
3e: Demonstrating Flexibility and Responsiveness   0 1 2 3 4

DOMAIN 4: Professional Responsibilities

4a: Reflecting on Teaching	0	1	2	3	4
4b: Maintaining Accurate Records	0	1	2	3	4
4c: Communicating with Families	0	1	2	3	4
4d: Participating in the Professional Community	0	1	2	3	4
4e: Growing and Developing Professionally	0	1	2	3	4
4f: Showing Professionalism	0	1	2	3	4

In a few sentences, describe how coaching has contributed to your growth as an educator since school started. Candor and examples are welcome!

_____

_____

_____

_____

_____

_____

_____

In a few sentences, identify one to three of the previous elements that you would like to really focus on developing through coaching. Why are these areas important to you and how do you envision working on them with your coach?

_____

_____

_____

_____

_____

_____

_____

Do you have any other comments? Feel free to use this space for open-ended reflection.

_____

_____

_____

_____

_____

_____

_____

CHAPTER SEVEN
Using Academic Interventions Effectively

As you work to improve and transform your school, important questions you must ask and answer are:

- How will you use data, observation, and evaluation to conduct targeted academic interventions in the classroom?
- How will you tailor and implement these interventions to raise student scores overall and boost achievement in particular subject areas?

Scores are important, but they show only the results, not the process behind the results. This chapter focuses on the processes behind raising student scores.

When we talk about academic interventions, we're talking about putting supports in place for students who have not yet mastered a certain skill or who have certain deficits. My thinking on interventions has changed over the years. In the past, intervention was only for those students who were headed toward special education. Now, however, without implementing interventions for most of the student body, it can be very difficult for most schools to get everyone working at or above grade level.

More and more students come into the classrooms working below their grade levels. They may not have disabilities or be in need of specialized services, but due to various factors they *do* have big gaps in academic performance. I believe that we are moving toward the day when almost every student, and not just those receiving special education services, will have an individual learning plan specific to his academic needs, based on his data. In Chicago, we've already taken steps in that direction. My school has served as a pilot for this type of approach, with a cluster of students receiving individual learning plans in either literacy or math. At some point, all of our students may be on individualized plans. That's the kind of radical intervention needed today on a schoolwide basis.

Intervention and the Three Tiers

To become a school where at least 90 percent of students are meeting or exceeding standards, you must put targeted interventions in place. Otherwise, academic gaps will widen. Students will always be behind if no one helps them catch up.

If you don't already use a tiered system of intervention, I recommend implementing one, such as Response to Intervention (RTI), to address the learning and behavioral needs of students. In Chicago, we have used RTI but are now shifting to Multi-Tier System of Supports (MTSS) to address the academic, social, emotional, and behavioral development of our students. Under MTSS, half of the interventions are for behavior, the other half are academic, and both are tiered. Whatever approach you decide to use in your school, I believe that the idea of tiers is a clear, practical, and helpful way to assess what students need and to systematically meet those needs through targeted intervention. You can adapt academic interventions to your students' academic needs in the same way that you might adapt PBIS to cultural and behavioral needs.

In general, these systems define three tiers. Tier 1 instruction will include those interventions and teaching practices that teachers put in place with all students. These include differentiation and scaffolding, as well as targeted small-group work and other research-based techniques. This type of intervention and instruction happens in general education classrooms every day.

Tier 2 targets interventions to students who have not mastered a specific skill or passed an assessment after receiving Tier 1 interventions and instruction. You and your teachers need to provide these students with more assistance. A teacher might bring together a targeted group—for example, four or five students who have similar skill deficits and didn't pass a certain test—and reteach or adapt the intervention so the students will master the skill and achieve better results with a new assessment. Tier 2 interventions can also include some one-on-one teaching, or the use of online programs such as Read 180, a specific intervention program for students who are reading below grade level and have not yet mastered foundational skills. Students in Tier 2 will be in the general classroom some of the time, but are also likely to receive some instruction with a specialist outside the general classroom.

Tier 3 is typically made up of those students who have Individualized Education Plans (IEPs), and at least some instruction for these students—and possibly most of it—will take place outside the general classroom. Many factors could cause a student to be in the Tier 3 category, but by the time a student does reach Tier 3, most general education solutions and interventions have been exhausted, and the student is still not working at grade level. Additionally, you have the data and research to support the decision to move a student to Tier 3, or to keep him there. At this point you put together the clinicians—the social worker, the nurse, the school psychologist, along with the parent(s) and the general ed teacher—to look for more supports outside the classroom that your team can put in place for the child.

In most schools, Tier 1 will be your largest group of students—probably about 80 percent of the student body—with smaller groups of students in Tier 2 and Tier 3. While this varies from school to school, 5 percent in Tier 3 is about average. However, there are schools where it could be significantly higher or lower, such as specialty schools that deal with social, emotional, and psychological problems.

Whatever your school's percentages are, you'll need to consider and support all your students. However, on a day-to-day basis, your primary focus is likely to be on the students in Tier 1 and Tier 2. Many guidelines and legal protocols are in place to help students in Tier 3 succeed. Those detailed measures and safeguards don't exist for Tiers 1 and 2. You don't want more students in Tier 1 slipping into Tier 2, and you don't want students in Tier 2 to stay there rather than being able to move into Tier 1. This can happen if classroom instruction isn't at the level it should be. That's why continuous and rigorous PD and intervention are so important.

When you get down to the details of planning interventions for all tiers, you need to answer a number of crucial questions:

- How will you choose which interventions to use?
- What is your process for implementing interventions?
- How are you evaluating the success of the interventions and adapting them if needed?

As you hone your procedures, you may also look to companies and websites that provide research-based interventions, such as Burst and Easy CBM. Once you've chosen the interventions you'll begin with, you'll need to ensure that all teachers understand their implementation. You can't simply refer teachers to websites and hope all goes well. Be sure to build this training into your PD plan for the year.

A Five-Step Process for Conducting Interventions

I recommend following these five basic steps in conducting interventions:

1. Make sure there is documentation.
2. Obtain the right data over a six- to eight-week period.
3. Be prescriptive. If a student's challenge is with letter recognition, for instance, you need a research-based intervention addressing that specific issue.
4. Collect data during the intervention to measure the student's progress toward reaching mastery.
5. If the student does not reach mastery, begin the process again.

As the administrator, you have to know your students' strengths and needs, and you have to monitor the intervention process closely.

You and your teachers will find, as part of introducing an intervention process, that some parents will immediately request that their children be tested for special ed. I find it helps to remind both teachers and parents that special ed is a process. The days of automatically putting students in special ed are long gone. For many years, kids were placed in special ed who didn't belong there. Now, however, the priority is on providing the right services to the right students at the right time. A child might not be doing well in class because he needs glasses, a hearing aid, or something similar. Another student might need more one-on-one instruction, but not full-time special education services.

This approach represents a shift in thinking for many educators. To help make this shift, some school districts no longer use the term special education. For example, in Chicago we call these students diverse learners and hold the mindset that *everyone* is a diverse learner in one way or another. We need to make sure core instruction for all students is solid and high quality. Someone who is working below grade level—or simply below her ability—should not be referred to special education if you have not gone through a rigorous, data-driven intervention process.

And teachers *will* be dealing with diverse learners, including those who are not performing at grade level. In 2013, only 41 percent of U.S. public school students in fourth grade and 34 percent in eighth grade performed at or above proficient in mathematics. In the same year, only 34 percent of U.S. public school students performed at or above proficient in reading in both fourth and eighth grades, with the percentages in the states ranging from 17 percent to 48 percent.[6]

We need to make sure core instruction for all students is solid and high quality.

Recognizing and meeting the need for focused, research-based interventions will also change your approach to PD. Some PD will be focused on general classroom instruction, while other aspects of professional development will be targeted to intervention.

You may want to focus some PD meetings on certain interventions, such as Compass Learning, which provides K–12 learning acceleration software. Another example would be a Text and Reading Comprehension (TRC) DIBELS (Dynamic Indicators of Basic Early Literacy Skills) PD for K–2 teachers. If you're using these types of programs, you need to make sure teachers understand them thoroughly and not assume they know how to get the most out of them.

At other times, you will focus PD on core instruction. How will you help a fifth-grade teacher who has a student working at a second-grade level in her room? What types of things does the teacher need to know, understand, and do in order not to be frustrated with that child? What kinds of things do you need to remind her of in PD, so that she doesn't just teach to the students who *are* working at a fifth-grade level? Maybe you'll focus a PD session on addressing lower-level skills through core curriculum. You may remind teachers to use guided practice and modeling for students.

However you direct your PD, teachers must accept that whole-group instruction is largely a thing of the past except when introducing a topic or a specific concept. Therefore, you must make sure that the PD you provide equips your teachers to deal with all of the varying ability levels in the classroom.

---

[6] National Assessment of Educational Progress, "2013 Mathematics and Reading," *The Nation's Report Card,* 2013 (nationsreportcard.gov/reading_math_2013).

Using the Data to Develop an Intervention Plan

As an administrator, you really have to pay attention to student performance at the micro-level. When you home in on very specific pieces of data, it will be much easier to craft sound academic interventions than if you're looking at 500 pieces of information.

By taking a close look at your data, you can move students into targeted groups for intervention based on their scores. If you're assessing the right data, it should tell you what skills or content certain students need to work on and then which groups of students need the same things. You can use this data to help you arrange students into small groups for targeted interventions.

Exactly what data you use to determine whether an intervention is needed or working will depend on your school, your district, and your regional standards. In my school, we consistently look at DIBELS data, Graybook (a database that allows teachers to access data about student participation and attendance), Lexile levels, and vocabulary scores. There are many ways to assess data.

As you begin analyzing the data and developing interventions, you may realize that you need to make a big change in structure or practices. If this is the case—and especially if changes will require some teachers to go outside their areas of content expertise—you'll want to assemble an intervention planning team consisting of you, other administrators, a coach, and a couple of teachers. You'll need to look at who can conduct which interventions, and who will be most comfortable doing what.

Next, present your plan to teachers and familiarize them with what you're thinking. Getting buy-in from them may take a few meetings. You can't craft these intervention plans in isolation from your staff and then just tell teachers to do it. Your staff will always have questions, and they'll need you to provide some clarity about your goals and methods. I recommend being as clear and open with staff as possible and willing to answer their questions honestly.

When you discuss academic interventions with staff, you're likely to find that newer teachers are, overall, prepared for classrooms where not all students are at grade level. More seasoned teachers sometimes aren't as prepared for that reality and push back against schoolwide intervention plans and new ways of grouping students and delivering instruction, especially if they've been teaching the same grade or content for a while. They may be inclined to do the same things each and every year. When you throw a curve ball at them by requiring them to take specific, targeted steps to meet the needs of students who aren't working at grade level, that challenges their expectations and routine, and can frustrate them or make them uneasy.

You can work with these teachers and show them why the changes you're proposing are important by continuing to have data conversations with them. The fact is that everyone in your school is on the hook for a certain percentage of students making grade level each year.

During these data conversations, focus on those students not working at grade level. Ask teachers: "Who can you get to make attainment? Who can you get to show really significant growth?" This is a crucial issue because, unfortunately, some teachers don't want to take responsibility for all of their students. They want to own the high performers, but not the low performers. It may not be easy, but you cannot permit a teacher to tell you that a student is simply not going to improve. The teacher must demonstrate exactly what he is doing to address the problem, in concrete and detailed terms.

Consider requiring your teachers to create binders in which they document, on a weekly basis, their interventions for each child. What skill deficit is being addressed? Who mastered the assessment? Who didn't? What are the next planned interventions?

In my school, I especially focused on this kind of weekly documentation in K–2 to build a solid foundation for the school. The more we could attack the gaps at the K–2 level, the better able we would be to produce students who performed at grade level and were ready for the high stakes assessments to come.

In the end, what's crucial is that teachers own their data. By that I mean that teachers have to move beyond blaming the student (or the parents) for poor classroom performance, and get past the old excuses or complaints: "These students are just not into school," or "The parents provide no support at home," or "What was the teacher in the grade level below me doing? Why are they behind?"

As teachers take this step, you will need to talk about what their data shows, and—when it's not up to par—about what teachers will do in response. These conversations can be difficult to have, but they are powerful in getting teachers to take responsibility in talking about engagement and rigor. Instead of casting blame, your conversations need to focus on core instruction: on why today's lesson worked, or, if it did not, on what can be done to improve it. What should we be teaching students in second grade? In third grade? How do we best prepare them for the next grade?

By requiring teachers to own the data—and not just their own, but everyone else's—you open the door to great things happening in your school. You can focus on exactly how you're going to move students forward.

Spread Intervention Among Your Entire Staff

How you handle interventions will depend largely on your school's staff and budget. Some schools have the budget to hire interventionists. My approach, dictated in part by my school's limited resources, has been to make everyone a part of the intervention process.

As with coaching teachers, intervention is a process you have to build with a team. It needs to become the responsibility of all teachers in your school. And it's especially important to focus on how the team works with Tier 2 students. General education teachers are responsible for Tier 1 interventions, and clinicians and other special support staff are responsible for Tier 3 interventions. Who, then, will be doing the Tier 2 interventions?

One way you can address this issue is by making teachers who are not in the gen ed classrooms—such as the physical education teacher and technology teacher—part of your intervention team. In my school, everyone takes on the role of a reading teacher at some point, and you can use similar strategies at your school.

For example, the P.E. teacher could, during a free period, take his five Tier 2 students to a classroom or the gym each day. Referring to his intervention binder, he can then work with these students on their needs outside of gym class. This same type of daily intervention can also be done by the technology teacher, music teacher, and art teacher. You can schedule these teachers' time so that, for instance, the physical education teacher is attached to Ms. Martin's second-grade classroom, and every day at 9:30 he will go to Ms. Martin's class and get his five students for forty-five minutes devoted to intervention.

It may seem, at first glance, that this approach is not realistic for you to implement in your school, but there are creative ways to make it happen. You don't need to ask your P.E. teacher to conduct interventions for large numbers of seventh or eighth graders. But you can ask him to conduct very basic K–2 interventions with small groups of five students, for twenty minutes at a time. This can be a workable approach in many, if not most, schools.

When everyone is a part of literacy and academic intervention, you're able to make the most of all your staff members. It has to be a schoolwide effort.

Monitoring the Intervention Process

As an administrator, one of your biggest challenges is monitoring the intervention process. Effective monitoring means you have to know your students, which is another aspect of your role as an intentional instructional leader. It also requires you to be familiar with the ins and outs of interventions, assignments, and assessments.

If you, as administrator, don't monitor to ensure that interventions are put in place and implemented with fidelity, students working below grade level will stay there. So be sure to have ongoing conversations with teachers: "What's happening with Mary Jones? I notice that she's still in the red with word recognition. Let me see the interventions you've provided for this student."

In short, what doesn't get monitored doesn't get done. This is true in every aspect of school administration, and it is particularly true in academic interventions.

Monitoring also means having the right people on staff and using them as a team. The detailed data on interventions, progress, and assessments add up to a lot to keep track of. You might identify a lead teacher to be responsible for monitoring, but you'll still need to have weekly conversations with teachers about monitoring assessments and being accountable for them.

You should also look at data weekly to see who's making progress, and who's been given an intervention and then reassessed. Then you'll be able to say to Mr. Fuentes: "Here's your printout. I notice you still have five students in the red. Talk to me about what those five interventions look like. What's the plan for these five students? What will you be doing next week and the week after that?" That's what an instructional leader does.

There are many tools you can use to assess and track student performance. In my school, for instance, we use the NWEA Measures of Academic Progress (MAP) for grades three through eight. NWEA has a continuum of learning called DesCartes, which helps teachers gauge gaps between what a student is ready to learn and what the curriculum is presenting. Armed with this knowledge, teachers can develop goals and design instruction to help close the gaps.

When monitoring shows that a student's scores aren't where you want them to be, keep digging into the data to find out the skills that this particular student needs to master in order to progress. You can say to your teachers: "What's the action plan for moving these students to the next score level? What skills are you going to teach and what interventions are you going to put in place so that they continue to progress?"

You can develop various tools, forms, and systems to help monitor progress with interventions. Figures 11 and 12 on this page and the next show two examples of forms we use in my school to gauge student progress on NWEA RIT scores (the measure we use in Chicago).

FIGURE 11: CLASSROOM STUDENT GROWTH TARGETS

School: Great School Academy   **Teacher Name:** Mrs. Smith   **Grade:** 3
Content Area: Reading   **Date:** October 7

Class Goals: Making Expected Gains; Reaching Attainment (at or above grade level)

Student Name	SY16 Spring RIT	SY16 Growth Target Met?	SY17 Projected RIT	Status Norm RIT (end of year)	Expected Growth (difference between the projected RIT and the spring RIT)	Divergence (Difference between the end-of-year norm RIT and the projected RIT)
Mary Jones	174	No (-7)	188	199	14	-11
Anthony Gray	200	Yes (+11)	210	199	10	+11

FIGURE 12: **TARGETED INSTRUCTION ACTION PLAN EXAMPLE**

This action plan instructs the teacher in analyzing data and grouping students, so teachers can identify students in need of small-group instruction.

School: Great School Academy   **Teacher Name:** Mrs. Smith   **Grade:** 3
Content Area: Reading   **Date:** October 7

Use the NWEA Class Breakdown Report to retrieve the student clusters that correspond to student goal RIT ranges. Use DesCartes to highlight a small number of specific learning standards for each group. Consider what strategies you will use to provide targeted instruction that addresses the specific skills students need to learn to reach this quarter's targets and beyond. Select targeted instructional activities at the appropriate level of challenge and intensity and identify any instructional materials or texts required.

Student Name	Working below, at, or above grade level?	IEP?	Winter RIT Score	Spring RIT Score	Current Growth Projection	Based on the data, my plan of action is to develop and enhance these skills and concepts through targeted instruction
Mary Jones	At	No	212	214	2	**Literature:** Summarizes information in literary text with extensive dialogue **Informational Text:** Makes inferences as to the possible effects for a given action based on information contained in informational text **Foundational Skills/Vocabulary:** Determines the meaning of an adjective from information provided by the context of a sentence or short paragraph (less than 3 sentences)
Anthony Gray	Below	Yes	172	165	-7	**Literature:** Summarizes plot of a story **Informational Text:** Describes contrasts made in informational text **Foundational Skills/Vocabulary:** Infers meaning of an adjective based on the context given in a short paragraph

These types of data and monitoring are useful for all students, but may become especially crucial if a student may move into special education. In the past, a child in the fifth grade who was working at a second-grade level would have automatically gone to special ed. Today, we're asking teachers to teach that student how to read, as opposed to making a referral. That child might still end up being a special ed student, but it won't happen automatically as it would have in the past. If the student is ultimately referred for special education services some of the first questions a clinician or other specialist is likely to ask include: What has the general education teacher been doing with this student? What interventions have been tried? What has the teacher done over the last six to eight weeks to indicate that she's worked with the student, but still has not achieved better results? There must be evidence for why the student hasn't improved.

DON'T OVERLOOK CLASSROOM ASSIGNMENTS AND EXAMS

In today's testing environment, administrators often tend to focus on standardized tests and assessments. Obviously, these are important pieces of the data puzzle. But you also need to pay careful attention to classroom assignments, exams, and quizzes. Looking at a sampling of these will tell you what's happening in the classroom on a day-to-day basis.

It's especially important to look at those assignments because not every child does well on standardized tests. When you put a time clock on students and put them in a room where everybody's being tested, some will get nervous or think they have to be the first person to finish. If someone finishes before them, they can think, "Am I the last person? I need to hurry up."

These are just some of the many factors around high stakes assessments that you have to be mindful of. To see the bigger picture, you can take a look at classroom work on a regular basis and get a more realistic idea of how well a child is doing overall. Is she completing the homework? Are the student's assignments showing a mastery level of 80 percent or better? What are her quiz scores like?

If you see that a student is doing better on classroom assignments than on the assessments, you can make classroom adjustments to help her. Sharing this information with clinicians may help them note discrepancies and make suggestions: "We noticed that on this particular assignment or on this particular quiz, she showed improvement. Could it be that you need to adjust when she takes the test? Could it be that she needs to be in a smaller group setting? Or does she need to work alone?"

By taking a look at what's happening in the classroom, you can make adjustments and see better results for students.

You'll probably need to delegate teams to help carry out all this monitoring; it's highly unlikely that you will be able to look at everybody's work samples. You simply won't have the time. This is just another reason that forming a strong ILT is crucial.

Common Challenges in Tier 3 Interventions

When students with the most severe needs are referred for Tier 3 interventions, clinicians direct this process. This is an area where your teachers will almost definitely need training to fully understand the procedures. The way Tier 3 students are referred varies among schools and districts. But one thing is consistent: To move a student to Tier 3, you can't just say he belongs in special ed. You need data and documentation to support your belief that this child belongs in a diverse learning setting.

As this process gets underway, you'll likely work with a whole team of people who combine their expertise to evaluate a student's situation and needs. The team members and specialists involved could include a case manager, social worker, psychologist, nurse or doctor (for example, to do a screening to see if a child's reading challenges stem from vision issues), and others. The psychologist might conduct tests to assess the child's mental state. The social worker may ask about what's happening at home to try to gauge what factors outside the classroom are playing a part in academic performance. For instance, in my schools we noticed that a lot of students in the diverse learning setting had been frequently absent. It's not that good instruction wasn't happening—these students were simply missing it. Based on this team's observation and assessment, the team may decide that the child needs glasses or needs help coming to school every day, instead of being placed directly into special education or a diverse learning group.

Or, if a student has been missing instruction, the team might recommend working to provide him with as many supportive supplemental programs as possible, such as after-school programs or Saturday school to make up for the time he's missed. If the number of days missed has caused a great deficit in the student's learning, the clinicians may decide to move forward with some additional resources, too. But the first step should be to put that child in some program that will actively engage him in instruction.

Another factor that can lead to Tier 3 intervention is when a child enters school at a later age or hasn't attended a preschool. Sometimes you may have a seven-year-old in kindergarten because she's never been in school before. In some communities, another big factor is a great deal of transiency among families. Some students have been in three or four schools within a year or two, and as a result have severe foundational deficits.

On the other hand, an issue might have nothing to do with missing school or starting school late. A psychological assessment may find that a child can't multiply or can't focus or sit still. The recommendation might be sixty minutes of additional reading from a special ed teacher. Or the child may need to be in a self-contained special ed setting. And then the data and interventions have to be closely monitored.

Even when the team has agreed on a move to Tier 3, interventions at this level are never straightforward, because parents and teachers often have strong opinions about special ed. Some general education teachers may not want to admit that they can't help some of their students alone, while others insist that particular students belong in special education simply because they're challenging to teach. Many parents are adamant about getting their children help and are happy to agree to special education services if that's the best way. Other parents get upset when they hear their child has an IEP. They want no part of special ed.

Part of your job as an administrator is to change the way you, staff, students, and families think about special education services. In past years, many people tended to look down on special education classes. In the modern school, however, we recognize that some classrooms may look and sound different from other classrooms based on the special needs of the students, but that every student has unique strengths and unique deficits and deserves high-quality education tailored to his or her situation. It is true that students with more severe difficulties can bring challenges with them. Some teachers can become easily frustrated with students in Tier 3 and may ring your office a couple of times a day. When that happens, you can direct teachers back to the student's IEP. The student in question may be acting out due to his different abilities, and the teacher needs to be aware of that.

A teacher's behavior management plan for special needs students has to be different from what is used with general students in a regular classroom.

One way to support teachers and build their confidence is through co-teaching, in which a special education teacher and a general ed teacher conduct lessons together in the same classroom some of the time. Everyone is taught together, so the special ed students don't get singled out. This is another instance in which some teachers may feel you're pushing them out of their comfort zones. There must be training and instruction around this approach, with teachers planning together and really being collaborative, working as a team in the best interests of students. This requires careful guidance from you as the administrator.

It's also important that you monitor the quality of special education services in your school just as carefully as you monitor and assess general instruction. In part, that means you'll need to be present in classrooms to make sure there is equality among the grades and between general ed and special ed classrooms. Everything that you've purchased for your sixth-grade general ed classrooms should also be provided for your sixth-grade special ed students. Your special education teachers should not have to search for classroom materials on their own. In addition, if you aren't providing detailed guidance and standards, they may purchase materials that are of a lower quality than you would like.

Another way to monitor the quality of special education services and Tier 3 interventions at your school is during professional development and at grade-level meetings. Make sure your special education teachers bring in work samples and can tell you what they're planning to do for each student. In addition, you need to ensure that both gen ed and special ed teachers are abiding by what's in their students' IEPs.

Also pay close attention to conversations between special ed teachers and general ed teachers. You want these groups of teachers to collaborate and develop collegial working relationships. The last thing you want is to hear conversations like, "Those students don't belong to me."

You'll have to be really present in PD meetings and definitely sweat the small stuff. What do the grades look like for your special education students? What's the modified grading scale for them? Ensuring quality instruction for diverse learners—and addressing challenges early—means staying on top of the details.

Making Major Shifts in Practice

Once you have academic interventions in place, remember to keep tabs on when you might need to shake things up. The fact is that no school—of any demographic, whether in a wealthy district or one with a high rate of poverty—can have 90 percent of its students meeting or exceeding state standards unless it uses academic interventions in new and creative ways to address academic performance. This is what I call making "major shifts" in practice.

This requires that administrators look at instruction and teacher practices in a different way. You need to really push teachers' thinking in order to raise student performance. Boosting student achievement requires that administrators go beyond the standard interventions and devise their own.

At one of my schools, we developed such a plan to improve our instruction and practice. I looked at our data and knew we needed professional development to address literacy. So I planned for an entire year of PD in this area. We crafted out what the lessons should be, what the teacher should cover, the books and materials that should be used, and the anchor chart that the teacher should create. We did guided practice and modeling. We talked about approaches to reteaching. I didn't have all the people yet in place to facilitate it, but I had a plan for what PD would look like during the school year.

During my second year at this school, I developed a PD plan centered around a workshop aimed at balanced literacy. Each week in PD we discussed a different segment of the plan for implementation in classrooms. I gave teachers a focus or theme for the month that they worked on in their classrooms. I made presentations to our staff about raising our literacy scores, along with showing videos and providing them with professional readings. My goal was to connect my staff with the new vision I was putting before them.

I directed my staff to spend the next three weeks discussing what their shift in practice would be. By "shift in practice," I meant that I wanted them to start thinking outside the box, beyond what they normally did in their classrooms each day. I gave them some initial guidance, but it was up to them to come up with a plan. Our approach had to start from the bottom up, not top down. I told my teachers that there weren't right or wrong answers on this one. I wanted to give them total freedom in devising their approach. The shift they proposed didn't have to be huge, but it had to be big enough to help move us toward our goals.

The teachers decided to group students according to their assessment scores, not grade level, and teach those students together during the first period of every day. For example, in a higher performing group we might have a fifth grader performing above grade level working in the same room as an eighth grader. In a lower performing group we could have the reverse—an eighth grader sitting next to a sixth grader. Our "big shift," based on assessing the data and using PD to implement changes based on the data, was to group and teach students based on their specific needs and abilities, not their grade level.

This took a lot of courage on the part of the staff, because it's not a common approach. It was uncharted territory, and it can be scary to go beyond the norm. But going outside the box is what I asked them to do, and because we had built trust and collaboration through continuous PD, they came up with a fantastic, innovative idea. An educational consultant who was listening in on our PD conversations one day turned to me and said, "Evelyn, you guys have made it into the big leagues now! Most schools don't have these kinds of in-depth conversations about shifts in practice. Those that do are the ones that dramatically increase student achievement."

Another great idea proposed by my teachers was that they should each be able to teach in every subject area. We didn't have enough staff to allow every teacher to teach only in his or her content area. So the language arts/social studies teacher was committed to teaching math for the first period of the day and vice versa. It was "all hands on deck," and my teachers were willing to step out of their comfort zones. That was, in part, because the plan didn't come from me as a directive, but came from them, bottom up, through their collaborative efforts. The teachers wanted to see all our students succeed, and they pitched in any way they could.

This experience made me ask myself: Why were my teachers buying into this new and somewhat daring plan with such enthusiasm? The answer came back to visionary, intentional leadership—creating a professional

Be sure that your teachers feel their voices are being heard.

learning community bound by clear goals, procedures, and practices. You must provide that kind of leadership to create buy-in among your staff. And through this leadership, you'll inspire teamwork, creativity, and innovation that can achieve powerful results.

Keep Parents Informed About Interventions

It's important to educate and inform parents and caregivers about interventions. It can be sensitive to explain to parents that their child is working far below grade level, especially when families may have faced difficult or unstable circumstances that have prevented them from sending their child to school.

Schedule meetings with parents to point out things they can do at home to support learning and be part of their children's progress. Make it clear to parents that they have opportunities to visit, participate in, and volunteer in classrooms.

Keeping parents informed is especially crucial when children are referred for special education services. All parents need to be informed about interventions. But parents of students in Tier 3 who know the special ed regulations, understand IEPs, and are aware of their rights tend to be strong advocates for their children. And that's good—we want all parents to be advocates, whether or not their children have IEPs. We just want to make sure that parents have the correct information about why their children are in special ed, how the process works, and what their children will be learning.

FROM THE PRINCIPAL'S DESK

Despite your best efforts, not everyone will be willing or able to buy in to your vision. Because I have a large enrollment of kindergartners, I once wanted to move one of my third-grade teachers to kindergarten. She was not happy with the idea. I told her not to worry about it too much, and that it was still under consideration. I told her I'd keep her posted on any decision I made and why I made that decision.

However, she was still very resistant. It was her first year in the school and this idea was clearly too much too soon. But I believed she was a talented educator. So I didn't want her to get so overwhelmed that she was no longer a valuable asset to the school or me. In the end, I told her I would choose someone else, and she was greatly relieved. This situation ultimately built her trust in me, and as a result she was more prepared to give her buy-in later, when she felt more confident.

Be Realistic About Your Goals

As an instructional leader, your ultimate goal is to improve student performance. But as a general rule, be careful about doing too much too soon. Be considerate of new teachers who may not yet be accustomed to thinking outside the box. Some teachers will need time to acclimate to their students and to feel confident in their classrooms before you throw something extra at them.

And until you gain your staff's trust as an instructional leader who knows what she's talking about, you're probably going to face resistance. You need to present your staff with a very well-crafted and detailed plan. Who's going to be doing what? What's the timeframe for proposed changes? How many students will be involved? You build strong relationships with your staff when what you say and do can be trusted.

In addition, work to foster a sense of camaraderie among your staff as they prepare to make changes. If you make major shifts in practice, some teachers will probably be ready to jump in right away. But they'll also need to make allowances for those who don't yet feel comfortable with the shift. If someone isn't confident about teaching higher performing students, he could work with lower performing students. A teacher could be placed with a small group rather than a large class. Or teachers could team-teach to support one another, with one teacher handling most of the large-group instruction, and the other helping students one-on-one. As a team, your teachers will need to be adaptable and ready to support one another for the benefit of the whole school and all of your students.

I've seen circumstances where the pressure to raise student performance becomes too much for teachers. Their physical well-being can begin to suffer. Their absences increase. Staff morale drops. You can't afford for this to happen.

As a school leader you want to see change, but you also have to be realistic and flexible about achieving your goals. Be sure that your teachers feel their voices are being heard, and that they believe that the administration and their fellow teachers support them. When you've developed a collaborative, trusting relationship with and among your staff, you'll be able to propose realistic goals that your team will support.

Room for Reflection

ACADEMIC INTERVENTIONS

- What major challenges do you face in raising student achievement?

- What new approaches could you try after reading this chapter?

- List three goals for raising student achievement during the coming school year or term. How will you achieve them?

- At your school, how do you determine who will receive academic interventions?

- What types of supports has your school developed and implemented to reinforce academic interventions?

CHAPTER EIGHT
Working with Common Core State Standards

Since the introduction of the Common Core State Standards (CCSS) and their related assessments, many aspects of instruction and school leadership have had to shift to meet these new requirements. Feelings on the topic are strong, as you surely know. Personally, I support the standards. While I do think students are tested too much in today's schools, I also believe that Common Core standards will produce students who are better educated and more well-rounded. If I were to keep only a single major assessment, it would be one based on the Common Core. I believe these standards challenge our teachers and students to really know their content, to go beyond rote learning, and to use the higher order thinking and reasoning skills that characterize a quality education.

As an administrator, you'll need to address concerns about Common Core from both teachers and parents. You'll need to make sure that everyone understands the standards and what they require. And you'll have to be sure that your teachers have the training they need to feel confident and comfortable upholding those standards and preparing their students for assessments.

Even if your state has rejected the CCSS, you likely will still face key high-stakes assessments each year, and you can still apply much of the information and guidance in this chapter to whatever those assessments may be.

The Common Core is the "what," which is the same for everyone using the standards. The "how"—how you prepare students to master those standards—will be different for each school and administrator. But in general, the Common Core State Standards probably require more depth and rigor than your old state standards. Part of your job is helping teachers "unpack" these newer standards and learn how to teach them. That takes time. To help you do this, you'll probably want to put together a good team in all of your content areas and meet with them weekly to discuss exactly what you need to do for your students to master the standards. Key elements of your team's approach will be planning professional development, monitoring progress, and addressing concerns.

Professional Development and the Common Core

Part of your professional development program will need to be focused on meeting specific Common Core standards. For example, how might you shape literacy PD around the standards on drawing conclusions and citing text evidence? You'll still want to do PD focused on guided practicing, modeling, and optimal learning models. But you'll also need to spend time examining the Common Core standards and making sure that teachers understand everything that has to be covered for students to master them. Teachers need careful guidance and training in working with the standards.

A number of websites can help you move toward this goal. These sites have done a lot of the work for you already, and they can help your teachers get on board with various techniques and approaches. For instance, take a look at resources from the Council of Chief State School Officers (ccsso.org), videos from the Teaching Channel (teachingchannel.org/videos /understanding-the-common-core-standards), and standards information from the Oregon Department of Education (www.ode.state.or.us) and Illinois State Board of Education (isbe.net).

Of course, as is the case with any other type of academic intervention, it's not enough to simply direct teachers to these sites and expect students to perform well, especially as you build the higher order reasoning, critical thinking, and strong writing skills that Common Core assessments demand. You still need to meet on a weekly basis to take a look at the skills students need to master Common Core standards. Administrators have to engage staff in careful planning, and that will look different from school to school.

This is definitely a major shift in thinking and teaching for a lot of administrators and teachers. One of the first things you and your staff will want to do is familiarize yourselves with what each standard is asking. That's not so straightforward or easy to do. I remember pulling apart one specific standard and realizing all the different skills my students would have to master to meet that one standard.

As you look at each standard, carefully consider the kinds of materials teachers will need to support students at that level. In language arts, you might look at informational texts, vocabulary-building readings, grammar supports, and writing exercises. In math, you'd probably think about supplementing your curriculum to support problem solving and student explanations and communication. Students might need journals, math vocabulary resources, skill-based learning centers, and materials for math projects.

Common Core also highlights the benefits of networking with other educators and forming alliances with other schools. I encourage you to reach out to colleagues to see what they're doing and to exchange ideas, especially around PD related to preparing for the assessments. The biggest reason to network is because you want to see all students succeed, not just your own. Without this kind of intensive preparation, your students will be unprepared for the kind of high stakes assessment that Common Core entails.

FROM THE PRINCIPAL'S DESK

Common Core requires major shifts in both English language arts and math, and there may be concepts that are new to some teachers. For example, three shifts in math concern coherence, focus, and rigor. So keep digging into the details, and see what your teachers already understand and where they need further support. One year, during grade-level meetings, I gave my teachers a pop quiz on the math shifts, but only one teacher really knew what they were. Although my teachers understood rigor in math, they seemed fuzzy about coherence and focus.

That was an eye-opener for me. I realized that PD around Common Core had to be intensive and on-going, whether I was dealing with new or seasoned teachers. This emphasized the need to stay abreast of what Common Core demanded. If we didn't, students would slip through the cracks. So I focused PD on the math shifts required. I found videos and other online resources that talked about these shifts, and conducted PD around specific math practices throughout the year. In reviewing teachers' lesson plans, I looked for rigor in teaching to the math standards. Websites with useful content include EngageNY (engageny.org), the Teaching Channel (teachingchannel.org), and the Council of Chief State School Officers (ccsso.org).

Monitoring and Assessing Student Progress Toward Common Core Mastery

My school is part of a network that provides instructional support around Common Core. This network looks at the standards and creates a curriculum planning map that tells teachers what specific skills are required for each standard and how long they should teach those skills (usually for a one- to three-week period). Your school or district may have something similar. If it doesn't, you'll need to design and implement in-school assessments to make sure you're making the necessary progress as you prepare for the most important assessments. And even if your district does set certain requirements for instruction and assessment, you may want to institute measures that go beyond those requirements if you don't feel they are sufficient.

To help your students master the Common Core, I recommend conducting assessments every five weeks to see if you're on track toward your goals. These assessments can give you critical information about preparing for official Common Core assessments, particularly when it comes to letting teachers know what they need to reteach.

As with any other academic goal, it's crucial that you monitor the process of preparing for Common Core mastery. To do so, you can develop various forms to help you keep track of skills being taught, how students are demonstrating their knowledge, and how their mastery is being assessed. Figure 13, on the next page, shows one such tool we've used at my school. It lays out a ten-week plan, including details about weekly target skills, activities, and assessments. You might want a teacher to fill out a form like this for each content area—one for English language arts and one for mathematics.

Common Core Assessments and Reteaching

Reteaching is a key aspect of high-quality instruction and crucial to helping students reach goals. However, teachers don't always know *how* to reteach, and Common Core has exposed that gap. Too many teachers simply teach the skill in the same way after some time has passed. But that's not enough. Quality reteaching requires finding a new and different approach to delivering content. Teachers need to determine what kinds of learners they have in class. They have to dig deeper and provide new opportunities for each child to be successful, instead of presenting the same task that a student failed previously. Students who are struggling will probably fail again if they are simply taught a second time in the same way.

True Common Core mastery requires teachers to make shifts in how they approach reteaching. As a result, you may need to intensify your practice of monitoring teachers' grade books, as you look at why specific students failed

FIGURE 13: TEN-WEEK COMMON CORE SCOPE AND SEQUENCE TEMPLATE

Teacher _____

Date _____

Grade/Subject _____

	Objective What will students be expected to know and do? In this space, describe the knowledge, skills, and Common Core State Standards that will be taught and assessed each week, for each content area.	**Specific Skills Covered** *For example:* Ask and answer questions to demonstrate understanding of a text, referring explicitly to the text as the basis for the answers.	**Student Activities** What will students do to demonstrate learning? What products or performances will they complete? How will you ensure rigor in these activities?	**Assessment Tools** What assessment criteria or tools will you use to measure student progress and achievement?	**Accommodations** After looking at your data, create small groups of students who need more support mastering certain objectives and target skills for the week. Who is in each instructional small group?
Week 1					
Week 2					
Week 3					
Week 4					
Week 5					
Week 6					
Week 7					
Week 8					
Week 9					
Week 10					

an assessment. (At the end of this chapter, you'll find a Grade Book Monitoring Tool reproducible that you can use to help you with this task.) Keep tabs on teachers' reteaching skills and approaches. Ask teachers, "How did you reteach that skill? What approach did you use? How did the student react? What further adjustments do you need to make?"

If teachers are struggling with reteaching, make it a topic for PD. Consider discussing the question of when reteaching is needed and helping teachers learn to identify that need. Key cues signaling a time for reteaching might include:

- When a high percentage of students haven't mastered a skill
- When students don't know how to articulate and demonstrate their learning tasks
- When students don't understand the real-world relevance of a particular skill

True Common Core mastery requires teachers to make shifts in how they approach reteaching.

Also encourage teachers to consider the following ideas when they do determine that they need to reteach a topic or lesson:

- The way each student learns best, and how differentiation can meet all students' needs during reteaching
- How to use technology in new and different ways to present content
- Using tools such as graphic organizers, manipulatives, flashcards, and other visual aids
- Implementing peer tutoring as a way to reteach a lesson for greater or deeper understanding

Until Common Core came along, I don't think reteaching had changed in many years. That's one reason why I believe Common Core is helping create better teachers and students. It does require a lot of difficult preparation, especially if teachers have not been given the right tools to work with. Yet, at the same time, it can be easier in some ways to plan with teachers for Common Core assessments, because you all know exactly what you're planning for. You know the standards each grade level needs to master. If you aren't getting students to where you want them to be, you know that you have to change how you deliver instruction.

Seek Out Quality Resources for Teaching to the Common Core

It's fairly easy to know what the Common Core standards are. The work really starts when you have students who are far behind and need to catch up to those standards. Finding the right academic interventions, teaching materials, and other resources to both address academic gaps and pursue mastery of the standards can be challenging.

In our previous state assessments in Illinois, we had three or four approved packages for literacy or math preparation. But we found that many of these materials didn't meet the requirements of Common Core. They didn't have the necessary rigor, and my teachers struggled with that. You may run into a similar situation at your school. The fact is that you can't approach the Common Core with stale methods. You really have to revamp the curriculum on some level, which means that you and your teachers will have to be creative and consider new outside resources. And—especially at first—your teachers will need to be willing to spend quite a bit of time planning around Common Core. Again, it's not about the "what" but the "how."

You can consider a wide variety of software programs as you figure out the best "how" for your school. Examples include Measuring Up Live (measuringuplive.com). When teachers plug the target skills and standard into this program, it produces a customized assessment. Another option is Reading A–Z (readinga-z.com), which provides high-quality literacy passages for each grade level. Programs that help with math standards include Go Math! (hmhco.com) and Big Ideas (bigideasmath.com). Similarly, the EngageNY website (engageny.org) provides a lot of quality assistance around Common Core math standards.

Along with directing teachers to quality resources they can use with their students, you'll also need to closely monitor their use of these resources. Your ILT can help you with that responsibility. During PD meetings, share resources you've found with teachers and, in turn, ask them to share resources that have helped them. For instance, one of my teachers mentioned Newsela (newsela.com), a website for informational texts and current events. You can type in a topic, choose a grade level, and specify and choose an area of the Common Core ELA standards, and the site will return articles meeting those criteria. Another great resource for educators is the Marshall Memo (marshallmemo.com), which explores ideas and research in K–12 education. It's important to have ongoing conversations with your staff about resources and websites, which can be a springboard for news ideas around PD and preparing for Common Core standards.

Get Parents on Board with Common Core

In all likelihood, you will need to take proactive steps as an administrator to keep parents informed about Common Core, alleviate concerns, and ultimately get parents on board. Some will probably know at least a little bit about the Common Core already, while others may be completely unfamiliar with it. And among those who do know about the standards, some are likely to feel negatively about them. How do you deal with these issues?

First, it's important to help familiarize everyone with the standards and what they mean for your school, your practices, and your students. You might start by planning individual grade-level meetings for parents around Common Core. However, there's a lot to take in, and one meeting won't do the subject justice. I recommend holding one meeting per quarter. You might choose to break down these meetings by grade level, too, but not individually. That is, you could combine some grade levels here, both for efficiency's sake, and so that parents understand the big picture and how Common Core works across the grades.

While you probably won't get every parent to come out four times during the school year to discuss Common Core, offering this option gives you the chance to give your school's families a lot of quality information, while also giving parents the opportunity to ask questions of staff, as well as talking with each other.

In most cases, I've found that parents really want to know the basics: What their children need to know, according to these standards, to move on to the next grade level. And once they see the standards, many parents will want to know how they can help their children succeed. At meetings, be prepared to answer questions about these ideas. What kinds of things can families do at home to help their children improve? What kinds of books and materials could they purchase? Which websites might help their children master a particular standard? It's crucial to provide this kind of information to your parents.

In addition, when discussing Common Core, reiterate to parents that they must make sure their children are doing the homework. You can prepare a set of questions that you give out to parents during report card pickup to make sure they're interacting with teachers and asking the right kinds of questions. If a father simply asks, "How's Hector doing?" a teacher can simply answer, "Oh, he's doing well." But that doesn't really help a parent prepare his child for mastering Common Core standards. Prompt parents to ask more detailed questions about their students' performance, such as:

- What particular standard are you working on now?
- How is my child doing in that standard?
- Can I see my child's last assessment?
- Does my child need specific help in any area? How can the school provide the help he or she needs?
- What supports are in place for students with special needs?
- Is my child working at grade level? If not, what needs to be done?

In addition to helping parents ask productive questions, arm them with data. At your meetings with parents, try to give them copies of the end-of-the-year assessment for the grades their children are in, so they can see ahead of time the kinds of things their children need to know by the end of the school year. The more information you can share with parents, and the more you can convince them that Common Core will help their children become better learners, the more support you're likely to earn from them.

Ensure that Students and Parents Know and Understand Key Scores

I recommend requiring every parent and student to know their key assessment scores. For instance, in Chicago, the critical number is the NWEA RIT score. NWEA assesses students' knowledge of the Common Core standards, and the RIT score is a grade equivalent score. Students should not be told each other's scores, but it is important for each parent and student to know what the score really means. This provides students with a clear idea of where they are and enables parents to better help their children.

Additionally, in my experience, requiring parents to know their children's scores piques their interest and questions develop from that: "What does a particular score mean in terms of grade level?" "What can I do to help my child?" "Are there after-school programs or other opportunities I should investigate?" In general, I've found that many parents aren't necessarily interested in knowing the nitty-gritty details of the standards themselves, but instead want to focus on data and assessment. Similarly, parents may not be on top of every single assessment you and your teachers conduct throughout the year—nor do they need to be. But they should know and understand scores on the key Common Core assessments.

Throughout this process, be sure you're sending the message to students and parents that they need to be aware of their performance and how they need to improve. When the stakes are high, parents and students need all the information you can give them. Be open to their questions, and be honest in your answers.

Acknowledge Concerns About Assessments

A crucial issue affecting all schools today is how much assessment takes place. Parents are concerned about their children's success and also about their state of mind. Teachers feel overwhelmed by the pressure. Meanwhile, school districts and states are establishing strict guidelines and requirements. As an administrator, you're often the person caught in the middle. You can't necessarily go against what the district is mandating, but you also don't want your teachers and parents in an uproar. Often, the most valuable thing you can do is simply let parents and teachers know that you hear and understand their concerns.

Beyond this, you can work to help everyone understand that you're all in this together. Reiterate to teachers and parents that your priority has to be Common Core, because assessments based on it are so important to determining whether or not students are promoted. So that's where you'll probably need to put a lot of your energy.

In my view, however, there is far too much testing. An administrator has to ask: when do we have time to teach? Again, if it were up to me, I would restrict testing to Common Core assessments, but we're all subject to the mandates of our school districts. So within those mandates, do the best you can to alleviate the concerns of teachers and parents. Create forums where they can air their views and where you can make clear your own priorities for educational excellence.

Room for Reflection

COMMON CORE

- What do you see as the biggest challenge posed to your school by Common Core? How can you address this challenge?

- What new approaches will you take to help students master Common Core standards?

- How will you change your approach to PD to deal with Common Core mastery?

- What tools will you use to monitor students' progress toward Common Core mastery?

- How will you support parents' understanding of the Common Core State Standards?

GRADE BOOK MONITORING TOOL

Teacher _____

Grade _____ Content Area _____

Date _____

Elements of a High-Quality Grade Book *(Please check* **Evident** *or* **Not Evident** *for each of the following.)*	Evident	Not Evident
Common Core State Standards are posted, and student learning tasks are aligned with the CCSS.		
Comments:		
Four standards-based grades are posted per week (assignments, assessments, homework, and participation).		
Comments:		
Reteaching activities are planned and clearly defined.		
Comments:		
Category weights reflect the grading policy of the school or district.		
Comments:		
Percentage of classroom mastery is above 82%.		
Comments:		

Grade Book Category Weights		Grading Scale	
Assignments	20%	93–100	A
Homework	15%	87–92	B
Exams	30%	78–86	C
Quizzes	25%	70–77	D
Participation	10%	69 and Below	F

General Comments: _____

_____

_____

_____

_____

_____

_____

_____

_____

_____

Goals for Improvement: _____

_____

_____

_____

_____

_____

_____

_____

_____

_____

_____

Please address these goals by _____
(date)

Follow-up meeting to be held on _____
(date)

Principal's signature: _____

Date: _____

CHAPTER NINE

Building Quality Parent Partnerships

Building quality partnerships with parents is essential in improving school performance. However, involving parents in your school in a positive way can be challenging. At my current school, I have over 700 students. Yet at local school council meetings or general parent meetings, as few as fifty parents might be in attendance.

Your turnout from families may be higher or lower than this. In either case, it helps to remember that lack of parent involvement is due to a wide variety of factors. Some may not want to sit through hour-long meetings or feel the meetings aren't relevant to them or their children. Others might work multiple jobs or very long hours and struggle to find the time for school meetings. Some probably had miserable school experiences themselves and feel anxious or mistrustful about the very idea of walking into a school setting. (If that's the case, it's all the more important to emphasize that they can help make sure their children have better experiences.) Others are happy with the way the school is being run and don't see a need to be involved. Others might be recent immigrants who are still learning English and who may find it intimidating to come to school for a meeting.

Help your teachers be aware of the many circumstances parents may be dealing with, and remind them that when a parent doesn't show up, it doesn't necessarily mean that he or she is not concerned. At the same time, be sure that your school and staff are doing whatever you can to increase participation and educate families about the importance of attending meetings that are crucial to school performance.

As the administrator, you're ultimately the person in charge of outreach to parents. You don't have the luxury of delegating this responsibility. You have to ensure that teachers are doing their part to involve parents, and that they are engaged with you in an ongoing conversation about ways to do this. You must know that newsletters are going out on time and that the school website is up to date. Above all, you need to shoulder the responsibility of crafting a welcoming and consistent message letting parents know that they are your partners in their children's education.

Conduct Parent Surveys

One important way to stay in touch with your students' families is by conducting a parent survey at least once a year. Ask parents and caregivers about the culture of your school and whether they feel welcomed there. Do they trust the teachers? What kinds of conversations are they having with staff? Do they feel teachers are respectful toward them? Why or why not?

You can also use this survey to describe the ways parents can participate in school activities and ask them for their ideas, interests, and requests for additional opportunities. This type of outreach can help families realize they have a voice in school affairs, and it may improve their participation.

Provide a Range of Options for Involvement

One way you can encourage parents to be involved—while also showing that you are willing to cooperate with them to find options that work for them—is to offer a variety of ways for them to participate. They may not be able to go to a parent meeting, but perhaps they can attend an assembly, a parent advisory meeting, or a bilingual committee meeting. They can volunteer for a field trip, volunteer in the classroom, or participate in a school-wide activity of their choice.

One approach I recently implemented to boost parent participation was for members of my Bilingual Advisory Committee and Parents Advisory Committee to meet at museums and other cultural institutions in Chicago. This created an incentive for parents to participate, while they learned about opportunities for their children at the same time. Parents look forward to these educational trips, which provide them with a chance to bond. You could try something similar in your school, based on your community's resources, your school's culture, and your parents' interests—which you can learn from conducting parent surveys.

Communicate Consistently

It's important that you use a variety of methods to stay in touch with families and that you communicate on a regular basis. Some methods are probably already in place at your school, such as sending newsletters to parents. But when you're working to transform a school, it's crucial to go beyond the basics. Brainstorm with staff about new and innovative ways to engage families.

At the beginning of the school year, focus on connecting with parents right away, through a Back-to-School Day, a Back-to-School Barbecue, or something similar. Prepare something to give to parents at this event, such as school supplies or other items. Then, as the year goes on, sustain and build upon the connections you've created early on. Require teachers to create various events throughout the school year to keep parents informed, such as literacy night, math night, and a book fair.

In addition, your school needs to have a friendly and accessible online presence, including a website and accounts on social media platforms such as Twitter, Facebook, and Pinterest. If you like, you can also provide parents with a chance to receive text messages as well as phone messages from the school to keep families and kids informed about school news and events.

Continue to push your teachers to communicate with parents on a regular basis.

Also take steps to tailor your communication when appropriate. Some things will go out to everyone. For instance, I recommend sending out a newsletter and calendar to each parent or guardian every month. Follow that up with phone messages focused on items or events that need close attention, such as testing. In other cases, you can target messages to specific groups of parents, such as reminders about meetings for particular grade levels. This type of attention to detail will help parents feel that you are in touch with them and their students as individuals.

Continue to push your teachers to communicate with parents on a regular basis. Whether it's about academics, behavior, or just a short note saying that a child had a wonderful day in school, consistent communication will build trust with families. You may struggle to build that trust if you don't communicate consistently or if parents feel that you only contact them when you have bad news.

When things get busy, it can be easy to let parent communication fall by the wayside. But while it can seem like an "extra," it's truly essential to transforming your school.

Prompt Parent Questioning and Prepare Teachers to Respond

Try to equip parents to ask teachers meaningful questions, especially during report card pickup and progress report time. I suggest providing them with specific questions that go beyond asking, "How is my child doing?" (See page 176 for more examples of questions parents can ask teachers, specifically about Common Core mastery.) These prompts can help parents get a good understanding of what's happening in the classroom, which in turn helps them feel more engaged and more connected to their children's learning.

At the same time, you'll need to prepare teachers to respond to those questions, as well as to deal with difficult or sensitive situations. It's best not to assume that your teachers will know how to respond properly without training and modeling. So have teachers practice role-playing their responses to parents who may be upset about their students' grades or have other challenging reactions.

Figure 14, on pages 186–187, offers suggestions and information for conducting role plays, which you might do during PD in the month before you'll be having report card pickup or parent-teacher conferences, along with other PD centered around interacting with parents and guardians.

In addition, I recommend creating additional role-playing scenarios of your own, depending on your specific school culture, challenges, needs, and strengths. When you have completed these scenarios, invite teachers to discuss them. What did they learn? What concerns do they still have about conversations with parents?

Ensure That Parents Are Treated with Respect

Help your teachers understand the problems and concerns of parents, especially if your school is in a less affluent area. Adults have challenges and problems that should not be overlooked.

Throughout the school year, remind teachers to stay connected with parents, to be respectful toward them, and to try to understand their problems and their concerns. Emphasize that it's nonproductive for them to judge parents who fail to show for meetings.

You want your teachers to be mindful of those factors as they try to communicate with parents and get them involved. Ensure that parents are treated in a very warm and respectful way when they come to school. Parents and guardians are your partners. Send the message that you want to work together.

PARENT PARTNERSHIPS

- What is the biggest obstacle you face in improving parent participation?

- What ideas do you have for improving parent participation at your school?

- How can you improve teacher interaction with parents?

- What kind of information is it important to gather through your parent surveys? How can you tailor your surveys to be most effective and useful?

- How can you strengthen and diversify your communication with parents? What new ways and channels can you use to reach out to families?

FIGURE 14: **REPORT CARD PICKUP ROLE-PLAYING SCENARIOS AND CHECKLIST**

Each group will be assigned one of the following scenarios. You will have seven minutes to prepare two, two-minute skits. One will demonstrate an inappropriate response to the scenario and the other will show an appropriate response.

Examples of Inappropriate Responses
- Passing judgment on parents
- Belittling parents or their circumstances
- Placing blame
- Attacking their parenting skills
- Escalating an argument
- Using a sarcastic tone
- Disregarding parents' concerns or feelings
- Getting defensive

Examples of Appropriate Responses
- Demonstrating empathy while affirming the school's expectations
- Using questions to get a better understanding of the parent's viewpoint
- Offering solutions and referring parents to resources
- Emphasizing your desire to partner with them for the child's benefit
- Making a clear, factual, and nonjudgmental connection between specific problem behaviors and academic success
- Remaining calm and professional
- Positive framing
- Providing parents with data to support your assessment of the student
- Admitting honest mistakes
- Being willing to apologize, make changes, or adapt to a student's needs

Remember that no one is perfect and it's okay to be "human." Parents will appreciate genuine responses to their concerns.

SCENARIO #1

James is a student with excessive tardiness and absences. In addition, his parents are often late picking him up. You are concerned about possible signs of neglect such as poor hygiene. At progress reports, James was averaging a B in your class but now has dropped to a D.

How do you discuss these delicate issues with James's parents and encourage them to work with you to improve James's academic achievement?

SCENARIO #2

A group of your students' parents approach you at report card pickup, irate because of the homework packets that you send home. The parents feel that instructions are not clear and no predictable routine has been established. Further, students do not know what you expect them to do, and parents complain that they aren't seeing a logical progression to the assignments. The parents are also upset that after all of the work they invest in completing the packets, you don't return the graded packets to the students.

How do you respond to these parents? What steps can you take to make your homework process simpler for parents to understand? How can you regain parents' confidence in the school and your classroom procedures?

SCENARIO #3

Shanna's mom is upset and has requested a thirty-minute conference with you during report card pickup. She says she knows you don't like her child, and you pick on her every chance you get. Shanna says that every time a group of girls is talking, she is the only one who faces consequences, and you never let her go to the bathroom when she needs to.

How do you respond to this parent?

Report Card Pickup Checklist

_____	Sign-in sheet and pens
_____	Report cards for all students on your roster*
_____	Parent surveys
_____	Promotion policies (grades 3, 6, and 8)
_____	Student work folders with graded papers
_____	Classroom environment is clean and free of clutter
_____	Five chairs are placed outside the classroom door

*Report cards for students with five or more absences should be given to the principal to distribute.

Closing Comments

As we come to the conclusion of this book, I know that the work you do is just beginning. And I know that, as a school leader, you have a lot to juggle. That's why I want to restate my belief in the approach I've called "visionary school leadership." By making sure that everything you do as a school leader has a clear goal and is carried out through a systematic, consistent process, you can better balance your many responsibilities and in turn strengthen your school, support your teachers, and prepare your students for success.

I hope this book has given you specific ways to meet the challenges you face by implementing the proven, tested methods that I've successfully used as an administrator myself. I wrote *The Hands-On Guide to School Improvement* based on my years of experience—complete with plenty of trial and error—and I am optimistic that the real-world guidance I've provided will help you address your most pressing challenges, fill gaps in your practice, and transform your school from the inside out. From the small stuff that matters greatly, to the big picture of student achievement, to creating a culture of harmony and respect, to making instructional leadership the focal point of your daily routine, to inspiring staff, to connecting with parents, I am confident that you will succeed in improving your school. And I wish you the best along the way!

> "Intelligence plus character—that is the goal of true education."
> —*Martin Luther King Jr.*

References and Resources

BOOKS

Danielson, Charlotte. *Enhancing Professional Practice: A Framework for Teaching*. Alexandria, VA: ASCD, 2007. Based on PRAXIS III Classroom Performance Assessments criteria, this book offers twenty-two components for developing a successful teaching practice. Includes practical information on state standards, formative assessment, and school specialists.

Kelley, Patrick. *Teaching Smarter: An Unconventional Guide to Boosting Student Success*. Minneapolis: Free Spirit Publishing, 2015. A refreshingly frank handbook that shows teachers how to close the achievement gap in their classrooms while streamlining their work to yield maximum efficiency. Includes online digital content.

Kessler, Susan Stone, April M. Snodgrass, and Andrew T. Davis. *The Principal's Survival Guide: Where Do I Start? How Do I Succeed? When Do I Sleep?* Minneapolis: Free Spirit Publishing, 2015. A practical, straightforward school leadership resource for new and veteran principals and administrators that offers hands-on advice for leading a school successfully.

Lemov, Doug. *Teach Like a Champion 2.0: 62 Techniques that Put Students on the Path to College*. San Francisco, CA: Jossey-Bass, 2015. Learn how to teach like a champion with techniques and tricks for everything from classroom management to student engagement. Includes access to the teachlikeachampion.com online community, where educators can find videos and sample lesson plans.

Marzano, Robert J., Tony Frontier, and David Livingston. *Effective Supervision: Supporting the Art and Science of Teaching*. Alexandria, VA: ASCD, 2011. This book gives administrators at both the school and district level tools for supporting teachers and providing helpful, effective feedback.

Saphier, Jon, Mary Ann Haley-Speca, and Robert Gower. *The Skillful Teacher: Building Your Teaching Skills*. Acton, MA: Research for Better Teaching, 2008. Research and practitioner-developed approaches show teachers of all levels how to improve their practice and communicate effectively with students.

WEBSITES

burstbase.net
Companion website for educators using the Burst: Reading Early Literacy
Intervention with supplemental materials and resources. Access must be
requested.

compasslearning.com
Tools and resources to boost student success and streamline educators' work.
Take a short quiz to receive suggestions on a customized software package for
your students' needs. Information about each curriculum is available on the
website, and educators can request a personalized demo of any of the games
and curricula.

easycbm.com
An enhanced district assessment system designed by researchers at the
University of Oregon as an integral part of an RTI (Response to Intervention)
model. The website includes FAQs about the system.

elmousa.com
Information about ELMO classroom technology systems. The website includes
ideas on how to integrate ELMO technology in lessons, downloadable lesson
plan templates, and training for educators.

engageny.org
Current materials and resources related to NYSED Regents Reform Agenda.
Includes information and resources for educators on Common Core State
Standards, data driven instruction, planning a parent workshop, and
professional development. A "Parents and Families" section includes guides
to Common Core standards and links to online learning games and apps
for students.

marshallmemo.com
A weekly roundup of important ideas and research in K–12 education.
Download a sample issue on the website.

measuringuplive.com
This site provides information about Measuring Up Insight, which creates customized classroom assessments for grades 1–8. Resources for educators include
information on Common Core State Standards, written and video product
testimonials, and case studies of schools that have successfully implemented
Measuring Up assessment systems.

newsela.com

A site with free daily news and current events stories tailored for students at various Lexile levels and grade levels. Register for a free live demo to watch how you can use Newsela in the classroom.

orionsmind.com

Learn about small-group instruction based on theories of multiple intelligences and differentiated instruction curriculum. The website includes information about programs and professional development.

parcc.pearson.com

The Partnership for Assessment of Readiness for College and Careers (PARCC) is a group of states working together to develop a set of K–12 assessments. Their website includes information about manuals, training modules, and test preparation tools such as practice tests.

pbis.org

Information about Positive Behavioral Interventions and Supports for all levels. Blueprints and presentation slides are available at the site.

www.readinga-z.com

Thousands of Common Core–aligned resources and downloadable teacher materials to support student literacy. Educators can sign up online for a free trial of the complete software, or download free leveled reading samples and resources for strengthening skills in fluency and phonics.

responsiveclassroom.org

Responsive Classroom is a research-based behavior intervention system dealing with social-emotional skills. The website includes educator resources, research, and information on on-site services and workshops for schools and districts.

secondstep.org

This site is an online resource for schools and families using the Second Step program. An activation key from the Second Step kit is required to access the website, which includes online training, teaching, family resources, and videos and games for students.

tolerance.org/blog/talking-circles-restorative-justice-and-beyond

Information about talking circles and restorative justice programs from Teaching Tolerance. Classroom and professional development resources are available on the website.

Index

Page numbers in *italics* refer to figures; those in **bold** refer to reproducible forms.

Acknowledgments

Thank you to the Chicago Board of Education, the staff of Arnold Mireles Academy, Network 12, and the Academy of Urban School Leadership. To all teachers and administrators who sacrifice your time, energy, and money: You are unsung heroes who help shape the lives of children. I celebrate you!

Thank you also to my wonderful editor Al Desetta, and to Free Spirit Publishing for guiding my work and sharing their expertise in completing this book.

Finally, I've failed and struggled so many times but it's been those times when I was on my knees praying that I gained the strength to keep going . . . "All that I am and ever hope to be, I owe it all to Thee. To God Be the Glory!"

About the Author

After serving as an educator in the Chicago Public Schools for more than thirteen years, **Evelyn M. Randle-Robbins** became assistant principal of Howe School of Excellence, a K–8 school located on the west side of Chicago in a high-poverty, high-crime neighborhood. During her tenure as assistant principal from 2008 through 2010, Howe experienced tremendous growth in attendance, academic achievement, and parent involve-ment. From 2010 to 2012, Evelyn served as the principal at the Curtis School of Excellence, a K–8 school with 460 students, about 92 percent of whom were from low-income families. Almost closed in 2010 due to poor performance, by 2011 Curtis had 60 percent of students meeting standards, up from 46 percent the year before. Evelyn is currently the principal of the Arnold Mireles Academy in Chicago.

With her extensive experience at every level of school operations, Evelyn has both the theoretical knowledge and hands-on "know-how" to overcome the challenges of urban school transformation. Evelyn holds a master's of education in school leadership and supervision from Concordia University, as well as a master's in elementary education from Columbia College. She lives in Chicago with her family.

More Great Books from Free Spirit

The Common Sense Guide to the Common Core
Teacher-Tested Tools for Implementation
by Katherine McKnight, Ph.D.
240 pp., PB, 8½" x 11".
K–12 teachers, administrators, district leaders, curriculum directors, coaches, PLCs, preservice teachers, university professors.
Includes digital content.

The PBIS Team Handbook
Setting Expectations and Building Positive Behavior
by Beth Baker, M.S.Ed., and Char Ryan, Ph.D.
208 pp., PB, 8½" x 11".
K–12 PBIS coaches and team members, including special educators, teachers, paraprofessionals, school psychologists, social workers, counselors, administrators, parents, and other school staff members.
Includes digital content.

RTI Success
Proven Tools and Strategies for Schools and Classrooms
by Elizabeth Whitten, Ph.D., Kelli J. Esteves, Ed.D., and Alice Woodrow, Ed.D.
256 pp., PB, 8½" x 11".
Teachers and administrators, K–12.
Includes digital content.

Teaching Smarter
An Unconventional Guide to Boosting Student Success
by Patrick Kelley, M.A.
208 pp., PB, 7¼" x 9¼".
Middle school and high school teachers.
Includes digital content.

The Principal's Survival Guide
Where Do I Start? How Do I Succeed? When Do I Sleep?
by Susan Stone Kessler, Ed.D., April M. Snodgrass, M.Ed., and Andrew T. Davis, Ed.D.
208 pp., PB, 7¼" x 9¼".
Principals and administrators, K–12.

Everything a New Elementary School Teacher Really Needs to Know
(But Didn't Learn in College)
by Otis Kriegel
224 pp., PB, 6" x 7½".
New elementary teachers, preservice teachers, and administrators.

Interested in purchasing multiple quantities and receiving volume discounts?
Contact edsales@freespirit.com or call 1.800.735.7323 and ask for Education Sales.

Many Free Spirit authors are available for speaking engagements, workshops, and keynotes.
Contact speakers@freespirit.com or call 1.800.735.7323.

For pricing information, to place an order, or to request a free catalog, contact:

6325 Sandburg Road • Suite 100 • Golden Valley, MN 55427-3674
toll-free 800.735.7323 • local 612.338.2068 • fax 612.337.5050
help4kids@freespirit.com • www.freespirit.com